THE
RECONCILING
GOSPEL

THE RECONCILING GOSPEL

BY CULBERT G. RUTENBER

> "But he was wounded for our transgressions, he was bruised for our iniquities; the chastisement of our peace was upon him; and with his stripes we are healed."
>
> —*Isaiah 53:5*

PHILADELPHIA

THE JUDSON PRESS

CHICAGO   LOS ANGELES

FOREWORD

EVANGELISM IS PRECARIOUS BUSINESS. We face the frightful possibility of preaching "a different gospel" from the one to which the Bible bears witness, and of coming thereby under the awesome indictment, "let him be accursed" (Gal. 1:7-8). For Paul, this was a serious matter, a thing of life and death. It must be so for us also. We cannot assume. Clergy and laity alike must engage in the most serious study of the meaning of the gospel.

Dr. Culbert G. Rutenber shares his reflections with profound clarity, keeping in mind the laity for whom this is written. But as the great Karl Barth has insisted, every Christian must be a theologian in his own right and think through with a measure of coherence the great issues of the Christian faith. Hence, neither this nor any other book presumes to be a normative theology to be accepted with uncritical assent.

Written at the request of his denomination for use in its Schools of Evangelism, it speaks with pointed relevance to the evangelistic task of the church.

Dr. Rutenber reminds us that the Christian gospel is anchored in history in the event of the cross and resurrection of Jesus Christ. The gospel is the good news of what God has done for the redemption of the world. In a nation where "ninety per cent of the people who throng the churches think that Christianity is a religion of ideals, primarily interested in matters of right and wrong," the biblical accent of the redemptive deed of God must be recovered.

He recalls us also to the understanding of salvation as "restoration of relationships." Harmless as this sounds, it

5

is a hammer blow of God's judgment, for "no one can hope for salvation who is not willing to be right with God, his neighbor, and himself." We are ferreted out of the abstraction into which we escaped in our "salvation of the soul," and confronted with the hard reality of salvation as a new relationship in the living context of our daily life as worker, parent, citizen, consumer, neighbor, and friend. Evangelism then is the witness to the gospel of reconciliation in the midst of life's deepest involvements, and the vocation of every Christian is to witness where God has placed him in the world.

Perhaps the most crucial issue in evangelism is the question of the redeemed world. "Has the world been redeemed? Yes—and then again, No," says Dr. Rutenber. Granted that the "Yes" and "No" are both true, our usual locus of emphasis is on the "not yet," while the Bible's center of gravity is on what God has "already" done. We must recover the "Yes." In this light, "salvation is the power to be our true selves in the freedom wrought by Christ" or to become what we are by virtue of what God has done. Or, again in the striking words of this author: "Evangelism is the persistent effort to get people to take their blinders off and see where they are as inheritors of great possessions left them in the last will and testament of the Crucified One. Salvation is possessing one's possessions."

The author brings his clearest thinking and most prophetic passion to bear on a plaguing problem in American evangelism, the incredible ease with which we divide asunder what God has joined together, that is to say, evangelism and social action. "The term 'social implication of the gospel' should be abandoned," says Dr. Rutenber, for "on this view evangelism is the thing; social action is only an implication." He rightly insists that "social action is evangelism in one of its forms," for "evangelism is the proclamation in word,

6

deed, and fellowship-life of God's saving will and energy in Jesus Christ." When life is largely determined by massive social structures, and decisions are made corporately, and relationships become less personal, evangelism requires not only insight but involvement in the social structures; we stand alongside our vocational neighbor, and in the actual stress and strain of this identification, we seek to bear witness to Jesus Christ. Then again, in a politically conditioned era of a world in revolution, evangelism which fails to discern the action of Christ in the midst of this economic and political revolution and attempts to imprison the Lord of history in the ghetto of the church, would make Christianity what it is accused of being, an anachronism! Evangelism demands a new style of discerning action. Words are not enough.

Dr. Rutenber presented these lectures initially at the Evangelism and Bible Conference at Green Lake, Wisconsin, in the summer of 1958. They were not the usual academic lectures. They spoke to the condition of the conference delegates with great prophetic power. While the written word cannot completely retain the indescribable power of truth when it becomes alive in personality, this book to an unusual degree communicates the living contagion of a theologian who is also a preacher and an evangelist.

Jitsuo Morikawa, Secretary
Division of Evangelism
American Baptist Home Mission Societies
of the American Baptist Convention

April 3, 1960

CONTENTS

I WOULD HAVE WORDS WITH YOU, READER

TO BE EXACT, I would have over 50,000 words with you. And obviously only he that endures to the end shall be saved!

This book is a contribution to lay education. It is not the first, nor the best, nor the last in its line. Many interests, many concerns, and many skills are converging these days on the laymen. There is a reason: the church and its mission belong to the congregation.

While I was in the process of finishing this book I heard from my friend Dr. Henlee H. Barnette, of the Southern Baptist Theological Seminary, something of what he has been currently working on: a comparison of Aquinas, the famous Catholic thinker, with Calvin. He had found in Aquinas a view of faith which suggested that since the average member of the church cannot be expected to know all the ins and outs of the Christian gospel, he must put his trust in the expert, the priest of the church. Calvin, on the other hand, insisted that every church member must have his own personal faith in the person and ministry of Jesus Christ.

Here is a basic issue between Catholicism and Protestantism. A Catholic does not need to know for himself as long as he can trust the church and let it know for him. But for the Protestant this is an impossibility. As someone has said, just as no one else can take my bath for me, so no one else can have my faith for me. Protestantism is essentially and enduringly a lay movement.

If this is true, then a certain amount of education in the things of Christianity is of absolute importance for the mod-

11

ern layman. Without some theological understanding, the layman simply cannot function as a Christian, a _witnessing_ Christian, in the modern world. He must know something of what he speaks, of what he believes, of what the Christian faith is, and of that to which he witnesses.

It is as a contribution to this truth that this book is presented. I have tried to write it in language which is understandable, but I cannot swear that at every point I have succeeded. However, in one sense I do not apologize for this. A person who expects to read about the Christian faith at the same level that he follows the adventures of Little Orphan Annie is expecting something that he is not likely to find in any foreseeable future. The things of God and Christ cannot be reduced to the comic-strip level of communication without serious misunderstanding. But the problem of communicating the truths of the Faith today is complicated by the fact that the laity has so little knowledge of the Bible. While writing this, I noted in the newspaper that a minister in California had discovered to his dismay that the faithful members of his congregation could not pass an exam based on twenty simple questions about the Bible. Words like "regeneration," "justification," and "sanctification" sound like words from another planet to a generation reared on terms like "carburetor," "equation," and "television."

The purpose of this book is to explain the meaning of the Christian gospel in laymen's language. By the end of the first chapter, it will be quite clear what is included under the chapter headings of the rest. I only hope that no reader will get bogged down in that first chapter. It may be that the first chapter is the most difficult one, though not I hope very difficult at that. On the other hand, I am quite certain that the last chapter is not only the shortest (a virtue in its own right), but also the easiest to read; and I suspect that each chapter is easier than the preceding one. Perhaps I should encourage my reader by suggesting that he start with the last chapter first. But wherever he starts, I shall be most disappointed if he does not at least cover chapter three. Chapter three is the most controversial chapter, and controversy is surely one kind of contribution to one's education. As Irwin Edman (I think it was, or perhaps Will Durant) used to say, there is nothing so educational as a jar.

Before I commit the following pages to the mercy of God and the reader, I want to salute Rev. Vincent deGregoris for reading the manuscript while it was in preparation. He kept pace with me in my frantic haste to make the inexorable deadline, with the end in view of keeping me from making too many glaring errors.

Culbert G. Rutenber

Newton Centre, Mass,
June 1, 1960

1

THE TRUTH WE CONFESS

"I FIND MORE PROFIT in sermons on either good tempers or good works than in what is commonly called 'gospel sermons.' That term has now become a mere cant word; I wish none of our society would use it. It has no determinate meaning. Let but a pert, self-sufficient animal that has neither sense nor grace bawl out something about Christ or his blood or justification by faith and the hearers cry out: 'What a fine gospel sermon.' "[1]

The author of those words was no heretic, but one of the great evangelists of all times—John Wesley, the founder of Methodism. Clearly he was not against gospel preaching. He gave his life to it. But he was against that form of gospel preaching, so prevalent even in our day, which captures the gospel in slogans and proclaims it by leaping from one slogan to another as a man might leap from ice floe to ice floe.

Now the alternative to proclamation by slogan is proclamation by explained truth. Such proclamation engages the speaker in theology; and if what is proclaimed is the gospel of Christ, then the theology involved is the theology of the gospel. Such theology is unavoidable. It is also important, for since the Holy Spirit is the Spirit of truth as well as of power, there is a relationship between right thinking and right living.

[1] From *The Theology of Evangelism,* by Henry Cook. (London: The Carey Kingsgate Press, Ltd., 1951), p. 76f. Used by permission.

The gospel is the glory of the Christian faith. No other religion has a gospel. The word "gospel," of course, means good news. Both words are important. The fact that the news is *good* is a commentary on the nature of the God who has come to us in Christ. It is not enough that God incarnated himself in human flesh. What is decisive is the *character* of this God who "for us and for our sins" became man. It is "glad tidings" we announce because God is that kind of God.

But the word "news" is equally significant. On the one hand, news has to do with something that actually happens. If I say, "Have you heard the news? K— is dead"—and it turns out that he is nothing of the kind, then I am not reporting the news at all but only making a feeble joke, or else passing on some misinformation. News is something that happens as part of our time-space order. Thus to speak of the gospel as the good news of God's saving act in Jesus Christ is to speak about an event in history, something that is part of our human story, something that can be pinpointed at a particular place and a particular time. News is something that actually happens.

But that is not all. A multitude of things happen every day that are never recorded, never remembered, perhaps never particularly noticed. Why? Because they are of no importance to anyone. The *New York Times* boasts that it reports "all the news that's fit to print." It makes no pretense of telling everything that happened in the last twenty-four hours. Who could? But it tries to tell what is newsworthy; i.e., what is important enough to be recorded for the American public.

The description of the gospel as good news, then, is highly significant. As *news,* it suggests something important that really happened in history. As *good,* it suggests the character of the God who caused it to happen.

Now as soon as we have said this much we have begun to differentiate biblical Christianity from some common distortions of it. If Christianity has as its special concern an event in history, then Christianity is not sheer mysticism. Mysticism is a many-meanings word, but as I am using it here it refers to the belief that God can be savingly found immediately in the human heart—if you dig down deep enough—without any mediation. But this would make the cross of reconciliation of no effect. Such mysticism solves too simply the relation between holy God and sinful man.

For Christianity, there is between God and man a barrier of sin which can be broken down only from God's side. The breaking down of this barrier was effected through that bit of history which we call the gospel, and God is now found through Christ the mediator. In other words, Christianity, because of the gospel, is tied to a something-that-happened-once and we cannot speak simply of the flight of man's soul to God as though nothing had taken place of decisive significance in Palestine long ago. It is to protect this emphasis on the mediating factor of Christ in man's redemption that Paul speaks of union with Christ (a historical person) rather than union with God. Of course, union with Christ *is* union with God; but it is a *mediated* union, a union that ties us to a particular bit of history 2,000 years ago, and that is just the point.

But if a Christianity with a gospel at its core is not sheer mysticism, neither is it mere moralism. Dr. Sam Shoemaker is probably right when he says that 90 per cent of the people who throng our churches think that Christianity is a religion of ideals, primarily concerned with matters of right and wrong. But that only proves that 90 per cent of a people can be wrong. Christianity *is* concerned with right and wrong. Deeply so. But Christianity makes bad people good as a by-product; i.e., a by-product of making dead people (spiritually dead) live. To effect this, a deed of God, a gospel, is needed. The trouble with a religion which majors in moral matters is that it lacks any redemptive quality. It is merely hortatory. As Canon Wedel puts it: "Ideals cannot command. They will not punish, nor will they reward. Nor will they save. Modern man could people the stars with ideals and values—they will not leave their heavenly abode to rescue the weak or the lost."[2] Canon Wedel then adds that if Jesus had been a mere prophet and teacher, his demands might have been sad news—the sad news of man's failure ever to be worthy of fellowship with God.

Because Christianity is a religion that glories in a gospel, sheer mysticism cannot define it, mere moralism cannot exhaust it, nor can general truths be its differentiating characteristic. A general truth is a truth which is timeless and universal—like "God is good," "There is a hereafter," "The wicked are lost," and "God loves his creatures." These statements are certainly true, but as they stand, they are not enough for characterizing Christianity precisely. They are not enough, because they do not tell us anything about that something-that-happened, and it takes the latter to reach the core of Christianity. Because the gospel is news, real *news,* it cannot merely repeat truths that are already known —"God is love," "God is powerful," and similar ideas. Christianity is not a religion mainly of tremendous ideas, though its ideas are tremendous. To say that God cares for men is to propound a great idea. But to say that God cared so much for men that he did something about it through the death and resurrection of his Son Jesus Christ is to proclaim good news. What we preach are the wonderful works of God, not wonderful ideas about God.

[2] From *The Christianity of Main Street,* by Theodore Wedel. (Toronto: Brett-Macmillan, Ltd., 1950.) Used by permission.

This distinction may be important enough to underscore with an apt quotation:

> The clauses in the Apostles' Creed ("suffered under Pontius Pilate, was crucified, dead, and buried. The third . . ." etc.) teach not primarily that God is a saving God [which would be a general truth—C.G.R.], but that God, in the governorship of Pontius Pilate in Judea, has wrought salvation [an historical truth—C.G.R.]. The redemptiveness of God could have been taught, in principle, by anyone: it has, in fact been taught by many, including non-Christians: it is the claim made for the existence and unique significance of a particular set of historical facts that makes the distinctiveness.[3]

All that needs to be added is that the "set of historical facts" not only makes the distinctiveness but also creates the scandal of Christianity. It seems shocking to many that the Christian faith should be so closely tied to times and places. But that is the gospel, and it stems from the Christian belief that God takes a hand in what goes on in the world of men. Our God is a God who does things.

Yet for all its stress on times and places, the history with which Christianity is concerned is history with a difference. The death of Christ, for instance, is not a historical fact in quite the same way that the death of Hitler is a historical fact. Both happened at a particular time and place. But the moment in which Christ's death happened was a moment of time which was filled with eternity, as the moment of Hitler's death was not. It is this that gives the Christ-event its power and universal significance. It is not only that here was a person who was part of our human story. It is also that "God was in Christ, reconciling the world unto himself" (2 Cor. 5:19).

The power and pathos of the life and death of Christ is derived from the fact that, as someone has put it, there two careers merged—the career of sinning man and the career

[3] Prof. John F. Butler, quoted by Edmund Soper, in *The Inevitable Choice* (Nashville: Abingdon Press, Copyright, 1957), p. 75. Used by permission.

of caring God. Or, to change the figure, two lines which heretofore had been separate (though interacting) merged in Jesus Christ—the human line and the divine line. As we read the Old Testament the line of God's activity appears, as it were, above the line of man's activity. Man goes his sometimes sinning, sometimes repentant, way; and God— if you will forgive the figure—reaches down with his feet and kicks to pieces the monuments of man's pride, and then, when man repents, stoops down and with his own hands fashions a better arrangement. God intervenes in our human story, he destroys and he builds, but from above and outside, as it were. God is in heaven and man is on earth. But then something happens. The line of God and the line of man come together; the career of God and the career of man merge; and in the life of one person, and him the God-man, our Lord Jesus Christ, we can read both the story of God and the story of man.

This is why there are elements in the life of our Lord which are opaque to the secular historian. The historian can analyze and dissect the story of Jesus Christ so as to lay bare the causes of his death in the anger, frustration, and intrigue of his enemies. But no historical dissection can lay bare the God who was personally present in Christ, bearing in his own person "the intolerable burden of our human depravity." It is the eye of the believer, not the eye of the secular historian which can see that. The secular historian can see the human dimensions of the life of Christ, but he can never pierce to its divine dimensions. Only the eye of faith can see that far.

We have been exploring the character of the Christian faith as a religion of historical events with the end in view of suggesting something of what is meant by that phrase. But we have not asked the even more central question, "What is the gospel which we proclaim?" We noted at the beginning of this chapter that John Wesley had his doubts as to whether all the heralds of the gospel really knew what they were talking about. Perhaps the following discussion will indicate why some contemporary students of the New Testament have entertained similar doubts.

At the beginning of the fifteenth chapter of 1 Corinthians, Paul writes of the gospel in these terms: "For I delivered unto you first of all that which I also received, how that Christ died for our sins according to the scriptures; and that he was buried, and that he rose again the third day according to the scriptures." Here the gospel is defined as the death and resurrection of Christ for our sins. With this definition there cannot, indeed, be any quarrel. At the heart of the gospel is Christ's atoning death and victorious resurrection. This is why in the Apostles' Creed (". . . born of the Virgin Mary, suffered under Pontius Pilate . . .") the whole of our Lord's life, from his birth to his death, is taken care of by a comma!

But while we must affirm that Paul has put his finger on the core of the gospel, we can legitimately ask if Paul meant to be exhaustive and exclude all else from the definition. Here we must, for reasons which shall shortly appear, say No. To say this is not to subtract from the centrality of the cross and resurrection. Rather it is to put these in proper perspective. Another passage of Scripture, the tenth chapter of Hebrews, helps to give us this perspective. In that chapter, the offering of Christ for sin is compared with the offerings of the Old Testament, which are but images of the reality:

> In burnt offerings and sacrifices for sin thou hast had no pleasure. Then said I, Lo, I come (in the volume of the book it is written of me,) to do thy will, O God. . . . He taketh away the first, that he may establish the second. By the which will we are sanctified through the offering of the body of Jesus Christ once for all (Heb. 10:6-10).

We note from this passage that the mere death of Christ was not enough. If his death was all that was called for, then he could have been killed by Herod while yet in his infancy and the world would have been saved. His death acquires its redemptive quality from the life of perfect obedience which lay behind it and of which it was the final seal and climax. He offered himself sacrificially in a life of love and devotion before he offered himself in that final, supreme sacrifice for sin at Calvary. He was "obedient unto death, even the death of the cross" (Phil. 2:8). So his life is part of the total picture along with his death, and his life includes the things that he did as well as the words which he spoke. Death, life, deeds, words, resurrection—all are inextricably bound up with the good news of God's grace in Jesus Christ. And if we want to go back still farther, we can recall that to those shepherds on the Judean hills, the good news proclaimed by the angelic hosts was the Savior's *birth*. Surely the incarnation is part of the good news we preach. It gives meaning to the death and resurrection.

If we enlarge the term "gospel" to include (in their proper place) all that Christ was and did and said and suffered, we shall find ample precedent. Here, for example, is the opening verse of Mark's gospel: "The beginning of the gospel of Jesus Christ, the Son of God"—and immediately the author plunges into the ministry of our Lord, from his baptism on. Indeed the very headings which we give the first four books of the New Testament are significant. When we speak of the gospel according to Matthew, Mark, Luke, and John, what do we mean but the whole Christ-story according to Matthew, Mark, Luke, and John?

In confirmation of this enlargement of the idea of "gospel" to embrace the whole Christ-story, it is worthy of note that our Lord himself is the first gospel preacher mentioned in the New Testament. True, he did not preach the gospel in its fullness, as the apostles were to do later. How could he before his death? Or, to put it another way, how could he when he was meant not to *preach* the gospel, but to *be* the gospel? Nevertheless, the record is clear. Up to the limit of what it was possible, at that time, to make known, Christ preached the gospel: "Now after that John was put in prison, Jesus came into Galilee, preaching the gospel of the kingdom of God, and saying, the time is fulfilled, and the kingdom of God is at hand: repent ye, and believe the gospel" (Mark 1:14-15).

The gospel that Christ proclaimed was the coming of God's kingdom in his own person. In him, God was setting out to put right what was crooked and perverse. Thus Jesus claimed to forgive sins—a divine prerogative. He never said, "Thus saith the Lord," but rather, "I say unto you." He claimed to be, not merely a servant of God, but rather the son (Mark 12:1-12); to be the only one to know the secrets of the Father (Matt. 11:27); to be a greater than Jonah or Solomon (Matt. 12:41-42). He disclaimed any consciousness of sin. He taught that the presence of the Kingdom in their midst in his person created an inevitable crisis. Their reaction to him was their reaction to God and his Kingdom.

Our Lord proclaimed this fact not only in words but also in deeds. His miracles were God's challenge to the powers of darkness. This is especially clear in the casting out of demons. Thus in Matthew 12:28 our Lord remarks, "But if I cast out devils by the Spirit of God, then the kingdom of God is come unto you."

There was, therefore, no radical discontinuity with the stories of our Lord's life and ministry when the early church, after Christ's death and resurrection, identified the content of the gospel with Christ himself. "For we preach not ourselves, but Christ Jesus the Lord" (2 Cor. 4:5; see also Phil.

1:18; 2 Cor. 1:19, and many other passages). "The earliest community," writes Paul Scherer, "began to conceive him as the very religion which he came to bring, himself the Word and Deed of God in human history." And he continues:

> What he said was not Christianity; not even to the people who knew him as flesh and blood and bone; not to Peter, and not to Paul: he was Christianity. He was the object of the gospel, not the subject of it. And he is still. It was not with his prayers they had to do, nor with his sermons. They had to do with him. He never promised that he would take them to Another, sitting somewhere on the throne of the world. "Come unto me." He never offered \to show them Someone. "Have I been so long time with you, and yet hast thou not known me?"[4]

We have seen that in order to get the gospel of our Lord Jesus Christ into focus, we must enlarge its meaning in such a way as to include within the picture the life that preceded the atoning death and the triumphant resurrection. Nothing less than the whole Christ-story is our theme. But scarcely have we acquiesced in this enlargement than a surprise awaits us. We find we shall have to enlarge the picture still more; for the Christ-story is by no means done. The same Christ who then wrought so mightily for the salvation of men is still working mightily today for the same purpose. True, his earthly humiliation and death are behind him, but having "ascended to the right hand of God," he continues to be the Savior of men and the risen Lord of history. Nor is this all. His people, those who have entered into his saving grace, wait for yet a further episode in the Christ-story; namely, the time when the hidden Christ will become the revealed Christ and will bring to completion and consummation the kingdom of God and every tongue will confess his lordship to the glory of the Father. Thus the object

[4] From *The Plight of Freedom,* by Paul Scherer (New York: Harper and Brothers, Copyright, 1948), p. 49. Used by permission.

of our faith is not only the Christ who *was* but is also the Christ who *is* and the Christ who *will be*. And the gospel has not been understood or preached in its fullness until all three time-dimensions of the saving grace of our Lord are taken into consideration. "We preach not ourselves, but Christ Jesus the Lord"—the Christ who was, the Christ who is, and the Christ who will be.

That we are on the right track here when we find the wholeness and fullness of the gospel in Christ himself, is confirmed by an analysis of the earliest Christian creeds and confessions. Oscar Cullmann, in his little book, *Earliest Christian Confessions,* has shown that the earliest confession of the church, the confession which the church considered as the essential of their faith, was contained in the simple formula, "Jesus Christ is Lord." For this formula the early Christians gave their lives in martyrdom in their struggle against the Roman Empire. They could not call the emperor "Lord," because there was only one Lord, Jesus Christ the Savior. Cullman goes on to show that the more developed creeds, with their references to God the Father and God the Holy Spirit emerged from this formula. That is to say, belief in God the Father and in the Holy Spirit was because of and through belief in Christ. The Father was the Father of Jesus Christ, the one who had raised him from the dead; the Holy Spirit was the one who witnesses to what Christ had done and makes him real to the believing heart.

Now the formula, "Jesus Christ is Lord," speaks in the present tense. But it implies the past and future tenses also. He is Lord now because he was crucified, risen, and exalted to the Father's right hand, there to wield the power of God. Similarly, because he is the Lord now, with all powers and authorities subject to him, he will be tomorrow's fully revealed and fully triumphant Lord in the final stage of all things. It is all this that F. W. Dillistone had in mind when he wrote, interpreting the mind of Paul: "Salvation involved a great deliverance in the past, a rich experience in the present, and a confident hope for the future—all made possible through the death and resurrection of Christ."[5]

We proclaim, then, to the world the tremendous news of the saving presence and activity of God in Jesus Christ—a whole Christ and not a half Christ. As P. T. Forsyth the famous British theologian puts it:

> It was God himself that came to us in Christ; it was nothing about God, even about his eternal essence or his excellent glory. It is God that is our salvation, and not the truth about God. And what Christ came to do was not to convince us even that God is love, but to be with us and in us as the loving God forever and ever. He came not to preach the living God but to be God our life; yes, not to preach even the loving God but to be the love that God forever is.[6]

Now the gospel as the saving presence and activity of God in Jesus Christ has two prongs, corresponding to the two words "presence" and "activity." The word "presence" speaks to us of revelation and the word "activity" of redemption. The gospel is both revelatory and redemptive; it both makes clear and makes whole. It shows us what God is like at the same time that it makes us like God, in saving alteration. Jesus Christ is at one and the same time the Revealer of God and the Savior of men. And these two are one, for he reveals God in what he does. In Christ the divine love is effectively active for man's good and not merely symbolized for man's information. Such revelation-through-action is characteristically biblical. The Bible does not give a formal definition of God as a means of making clear the nature of God. Rather, its approach to God's nature is through the narrative of his acts. It is as though

[5] From *The Significance of the Cross,* by F. W. Dillistone (Philadelphia: The Westminster Press, Copyright, 1944), p. 48. Used by permission.
[6] From *The Person and Place of Jesus Christ,* by P. T. Forsyth (London: Hodder & Stoughton, 1910; Independent Press, 1946. Naperville, Ill.: Alec R. Allenson, Inc., 1948), p. 354. Used by permission.

the Bible said to us: "Do you want to know what God is like? Then let me tell you a story." The whole biblical record is that story, but its core and climax is the story of Jesus Christ. It is in him that we see God; and his gospel is thus revelation as well as redemption. To this revelation let us now turn, and let us ask ourselves the question, Who is the God whom Jesus Christ has made known?

Not to become too technical and inclusive, let us note merely three things that can be said about the God who has come to us in Jesus Christ. The first is, *God is the light that discloses* (see 1 John 1:5). To say that God is light is to say that God wills to show himself. "God is light" is just another way of saying that God is the self-revealing one. He is not seen in the light of something else. He is himself the light in which he is seen. This means that God can only be known through God. And if this sounds confusing, let us just leave it at this: that God's revelation of himself is in some sense self-authenticating. In his light we see—Him.

Now the *place* where God has chosen to make himself known is Jesus Christ. Thus Paul writes, "For God, who commanded the light to shine out of darkness, hath shined in our hearts, to give the light of the knowledge of the glory God in the face of Jesus Christ" (2 Cor. 4:6). Elsewhere Paul writes of God, "who hath delivered us from the power of darkness, and hath translated us into the kingdom of his dear Son . . . who is the image of the invisible God" (Col. 1:13-15).

The choice of Christ as the revelation of God is an expression of the dilemma of God. As personal, God must reveal himself to us in the things that he says and the way that he acts. But he must talk our language. A foreigner who addresses me in Japanese will not get very far. I do not speak that tongue. So, too, if God addresses me in some celestial way, I will not comprehend. If God wishes to communicate with me, he must speak in a language that I can understand, a human language. And this is exactly what God does. Jesus Christ is God getting down to where I live, talking and behaving in a human way which I can understand. The only thing I know from the inside is human life. Jesus Christ is God made human.

I have related elsewhere[7] the story of a man meditating in the woods. When he accidentally disturbed a couple of busy ants, they hastily fled in terror. "I'm not going to hurt you, little ants," the man murmured. But the ants paid no attention. They didn't speak English! Speculating idly, the man realized that if he were really to quiet their fears he would have to become an ant without ceasing to be the human being whose motives and intentions needed interpretation. He would have to lay hold of ant-ness with one hand and of human being-ness with the other, if he were to interpret the higher life to the lower. Then suddenly he realized that this was God's dilemma too, and that God solved it in Jesus Christ. As Dorothy Sayers puts it, the face of the living God was turned toward humanity and, lo, it was the face of a suffering and rejoicing man.

> I saw God bare His soul one day
> Where all the earth might see
> The stark and naked heart of Him
> On lonely Calvary.
>
> There was a crimson sky of blood
> And overhead a storm.
> When lightning slit the cloud a flood
> Of light engulfed His form.

[7] In *The Price and the Prize,* by Culbert G. Rutenber (Philadelphia: The Judson Press, 1953), p. 35.

Beyond the storm a rainbow lent
A light to every clod,
And on that cross mine eyes beheld
The naked soul of God.
                    — William L. Stidger[8]

In the light that God is, we not only see God but also
ourselves; and at the same point where the view into God's
heart is clearest, the view into man's heart is also clearest
—at the cross. This is not accidental. The Greeks used to
say, "Know thyself." But the Greeks had no idea how
difficult that injunction was. Today, with all that psychology
has taught us about the unconscious, mixed motives, ration-
alizations, the eye that will not see, etc., we know enough
about the murky depths of a man's soul to know how difficult self-knowledge is. Psychology can teach us much about
men, but there are some things that we can know about
man only in the presence of God. At the cross where the
revelation of God is most complete, the revelation of man is
also most complete.

At the cross we see man both in his actuality and in his
potentiality. Man in his actuality is revealed as the creature
that looks perfection in the face and then determines to
murder it. It is at the cross that we are unmasked for the
sinners that we are. We resent Christ. His goodness rebukes
us. We do not want God on his own terms; we want him
on our terms. As Forsyth says somewhere, we are neither
just stray sheep nor wandering pilgrims; we are rebels,
caught red-handed with the weapons in our hands. It is at
the cross that the sinfulness of sin is revealed. And we all
are guilty. The sins that crucified Christ—the cowardice,
envy, jealousy, conformity, greed, and selfishness—these
are in us all.

[8] "I Saw God Naked in the Night" by William L. Stidger. In *Redemption: An Anthology of the Cross,* edited by George Stewart (New York:
Harper & Brothers, Copyright, 1927), p. 275. Used by permission.

But if the Christian faith takes a very dim view of man in one sense, it takes a very high view of man in another sense. No religion paints man as he is, in his historical actuality, in blacker terms than does Christianity. Man is not only one who sins ("We all make mistakes once in a while. . . . I'm only human, after all"); man is a sinner at the very core of him. But in his potentiality, man is greater than he ever dreamed of. For by the grace of God a man can become like Jesus Christ, the victim of man's aggression but nonetheless the norm of true manhood. In the light of Jesus Christ we see both what we were—and are meant to be, and at the same time we behold the depth to which we have fallen.

The metaphor of light, then, means that God is the God of revelation. But what does God reveal himself to *be?* What is the nature of the God with whom we deal in the gospel? The answer to this is twofold: God is the fire that consumes and God is the love that redeems.

God as *the fire that consumes* (Heb. 12:29) is the God of judgment who takes us and his own will for us too seriously to let us sin with impunity. The judgment of God is usually associated with his holiness. His holiness means on the one hand his separateness, the fact that he is God and not man, Creator and not creature. God is the holy one, the Other. He is not the Man Upstairs, much like us only a couple of feet taller. He is the Different; and "the fear of the Lord" is the recognition of the distance between the God who is the holy Lord and ourselves.

But there is also a moral quality in the holiness of God. It is because God is holy that "the wrath of God is revealed from heaven against all ungodliness" (Rom. 1:18). The wrath of God must be taken with great seriousness, if the amazing goodness of his grace in Christ Jesus is to be even partly grasped. It is the holy wrath of God which keeps his love from being misunderstood as sentimentality. God is not "amiable," as a recent writer has judged him. His fatherhood is not to be misconstrued as grandpappyhood. He is not the good fellow of the *Rubáiyát* who winks at sin and does a porter's job around the place. God is the guardian of a moral universe in which whatever is sown is also reaped. He is resistant to the sinful resistance of man. He rejects man's rejection of love. He is the God of judgment who says a persistent and unwavering No! to all that is wrong and crooked in man. The cross is the revelation of the depth of God's judgment. Sin could not lightly be overlooked; it took *that* to handle it. God's holiness is the presupposition of love's activity. His delivering love in the gospel would not shine so brightly if the stakes were not so high, the moment not so dark, and the prospects not so bleak.

But God's love does shine. For God is not only the fire that consumes but also *the love that redeems.* He wills our deliverance, not our doom.

It is now widely understood that the language in which our New Testament was written has many names for love. Thus there is *eros. Eros* is craving love, the love of desire. *Eros* is awakened by some value, some wanted quality in the object of love. There is nothing sinful about *eros,* as such. God made us with desires and needs which we rightfully seek to meet. *Eros* easily becomes demonic, however, when linked to that sin in which we all share and whose nature is such that by virtue of it each seeks to make himself the center of the universe. Where each man seeks to appropriate to himself the limited goods of life, it is clear that trouble is unavoidable.

There is another Greek work for love—*philia. Philia* is the love between equals. In one of the later sections of the *Nicomachean Ethics,* Aristotle has one of the most moving

discussions of this type of love in all literature. He insists
that true friendship is only possible between good men who
share a common concern for goodness. Here again we must
point out that there is certainly a place in life for those rare,
intimate friendships that are based on common interests
and compatibilities. Marriage, in one aspect of it, is such a
relationship. It is an exclusive, intimate kind of relationship in which the many are not permitted to enter. It is
discriminating; one has time in life to cultivate only a few
really deep and co-sharing friendships.

But there is still another word for love, and it is the word
that the early Christians picked up from classical Greek
—a neutral, colorless, rarely used word—and filled with
Christ. It is the word *agapē*. This is the word used in the
New Testament for the love of God seen in Jesus Christ.
What those early Christians saw in Christ and his cross was
not *eros* (which is not to deny that he *had* his *eros*-
moments). It was not because they were the objects of a
craving desire which met his needs that Christ died for his
enemies. The distinctive thing about his love was not that
it was reserved for equals. Indeed, it was the scandal of his
ministry all along that instead of loving the righteous and
shrinking from the unrighteous (as any good man should)
he consorted with publicans and sinners, to the shocked
horror of the religious leaders. He offered his friendship,
not to those who *had* worth and value, but to those who had
none—to the harlots and the outcasts; not to equals (who
was his equal?) but to unequals. By his life with and death
for sinners, our Lord struck a blow at the contemporary
philosophy of religious love: love good people and avoid
bad people. It was this undiscriminating love, if you please,
for which the early Christians sought a label when they
reminted the word *agapē* and filled it with Christ the Lover,
who loved infinitely while being infinitely rejected. God is

agapē (1 John 4:8)! This is the simple, wonderful truth which Christianity affirms on the basis of revelation. The unlovely, unworthy sinner (and this includes us all) acquires worth because he is loved of God. God's love is a stooping, heedless, self-giving love aimed at the good of the beloved. It is not an emotion but an activity, a boundless energy of limitless goodwill.

To say that God is love is to say that love is creative. We who were made in the image of God were made in, through, and for love. Hydrogen bombs may have an unsurpassed destructive force, but only love is constructive and creative.

Then, because God is love, love is redemptive. Love seeks until it finds an entrance and mends what is broken, purifies what is corrupt, delivers what is bound, and redeems what is lost.

Finally, because God is love, love is the strongest thing in the world. To overthrow love would be to overthrow God. The omnipotence of God is not to be pictured on the analogy of a despot, who having a monopoly of power in his realm, can use that power in any arbitrary way he pleases. The omnipotence of God—let us be very clear about this— is the omnipotence of suffering, self-giving, stooping love. It is Christ crucified who is not only the *wisdom* of God but also the power of God (1 Cor. 1:24-25). It is of the greatest significance that the final triumph of God is depicted, at the end of the New Testament, as the triumph of the Lamb, the symbol of suffering innocence.

God is love. Therefore love is not an ideal to be pursued but a reality to be discovered. It is not something to be striven for, but something to be surrendered to. Indeed *agapē* is ultimate reality. Psychology has unearthed the enormous need and power of love in human relations. What Christianity does is to enlarge the perspective and ground the human in the cosmic. It is because love is rooted and grounded in the structure of the universe that on the human level it is "the hope of the world" (Karl Menninger). It is because love is the law of the universe that it is the law of our life and we must either "love or perish" (Smiley Blanton).

There now is need for some comment on the relation between God as "the fire that consumes" and God as "the love that redeems," for it is the core of the Christian idea of God that *both* of these aspects of the divine nature must be affirmed, however paradoxical that may sound. No understanding of the revelation of God is possible which loses sight of *either* truth. God's love is a holy love; his holiness is a loving holiness.

Perhaps some illumination of the relation between holiness and love, between wrath and redemption, may emerge if we recall that love and hate (interpreted as righteous indignation) are not opposites. Any kind of love which is indifferent to the fate and fortune of the beloved is obviously phony. Christian love does not dissolve righteous indignation; it heightens it. God is not indifferent to moral values; he supports and sustains them. It is because God loves so deeply and purely and intensely that he hates the sin which corrupts and perverts his creation. Furthermore, the intensity of God's hatred of sin is in direct proportion to the depth of his love. Thus we have the picture in the Book of Revelation of the wrath of the Lamb—not of the tiger or the lion, but of the *lamb,* the symbol of innocent suffering (Rev. 6:16-17).

But sin is not a "thing." You cannot measure it with a tape, nor weigh it by the pound, nor slice it into parts. Sin exists only as persons give it existence in their attitudes and actions. Sin is perversion of personality. Hence God's judgment on sin cannot fall on sin itself, as though sin itself were some entity, but must fall upon the sinner who actualizes it and gives it reality. This means we must take a close look at the famous phrase, "Hate the sin but love the sinner." Fortunately, there is a wonderful truth expressed in that phrase. But it is often stretched beyond valid bounds. It is a partial truth, because the sinner and his sin cannot be neatly separated in the way that a hat can be separated from the head. The sinner, in a very real sense, exists in and through his attitudes and actions. The sinner who is loved is the person who just gave himself to sinning, and the sin that is hated is the sin to which this person just gave expression. Sin and sinner are intertwined and cannot be separated. It is this fact which gives life its pathos and tragic aspect, both for us and for God. I cannot be abstracted from my sin, nor can my neighbor be abstracted from his; and God, who in his love wills to give so much, can be frustrated by our refusal to receive. At this point the sin that God hates inevitably determines the relationship and we know God only in his judgment, to our condemnation and to his infinite sorrow.

So much for the gospel as revelation. Let us turn now to the gospel as redemption, as the activity of God for the salvation of men. We shall be pursuing the meaning of the gospel as redemption throughout the next chapter. For the present, then, let us be satisfied with the mere fact of redemption, and let us note that it is this fact which gives to Christianity its air of finality and even what some people would call its intolerance.

In modern parlance, intolerance is a very bad word. It is associated with another very bad word—fanaticism. Tolerance, however, is a good word in modern parlance. It is associated with good taste, broadmindedness, and similar virtues. For many, evangelism and missionary activity smack of unendurable intolerance and fanaticism. The Hindu intellectual Dr. Krishnalal Shridharani speaks eloquently for this point of view:

> But I am opposed, on principle, to the whole idea of missionary evangelism. The very notion implies a superiority complex as well as an impulse of self-righteousness. Now that might be tolerable in other fields, but when it is brought into the realm of religion and the spirit, it looks very strange to the Hindu. To the Hindu philosopher, nothing is more irreligious than a holier-than-thou attitude—an attitude which of necessity provides the driving force of evangelism. One cannot describe it as a human desire to share with fellowmen things that are found personally precious. Such a desire would turn into fellowship, into discourse, never into a drive for conversion. In this respect I feel that all the great religions of the world have one thing to learn from Hinduism: a humility born of a profound philosophic insight into the relativity of knowledge, of ideals. According to Hinduism, Truth (God, the Cosmic Law, whatever is the cherished name) is one, but there are many approaches to it. Like the center of a circle it can be reached from a million different points. I think that in this Hinduism is more in harmony with the spirit of modern science than almost any other great religion. It is forgivable to insist on *one* God, but to insist upon *The* Prophet and *The* Law is intellectually wrong.

> Did you ever hear of any missionary movement for mass conversion that was based on any theory save that of *The* Prophet, *The* Son of God and *The* Way? This exclusiveness is antispiritual inasmuch as it is overweening in the light of the limitations of human perception. That is why Hinduism, of all the great religions of the world, has never organized a missionary movement. For there are not only different approaches to The Truth, but different approaches suit different peoples, and there can never be a totalitarian uniformity in spiritual pursuits. . . .[9]

Dr. Shridharani's view is typically Hindu. But it is by no means exclusively so. There are many churchmen in the West who share a similar feeling about the exclusivistic claims of Christianity, including such notables as Arnold

[9] Quoted in *Revelation and Evangelism*, by F. W. Dillistone (London: Lutterworth Press, 1948), p. 21-22. Used by permission.

Toynbee and W. E. Hocking. Obviously such a widely held view merits some examination.

It is, of course, immediately clear that self-righteous attitudes on the part of Christians and superiority complexes are wholly inappropriate and out of place—although it is certainly questionable if these have had any major influence in evangelism. But to avoid any suspicion of such attitudes, men like Hendrick Kraemer have preferred to say that we evangelize not because we have the truth, but because the Truth, namely Jesus Christ, has us and wills to have all men everywhere.

Similarly, it is apparent, surely, that what divides those who believe with Shridharani from those who do not is not the presence or absence of tolerance. What divides them is that the former group believes that there is no final truth of God, while the latter group believes that there is. Where all is relative and where we must be agnostic about ultimate truth, there is no virtue in being tolerant. There is nothing to be intolerant about. What is here called tolerance is merely the sophisticated agnosticism of those who believe that no one knows the truth or can know it. But where one believes that there is truth that is discoverable, he cannot be indifferent to error. The modern teacher of science cannot be indifferent as to whether his students believe in the caloric theory of heat of the 18th century or the modern theory. The man who believes that God has spoken cannot act as though God had not spoken.

Tolerance is the virtue of those who have great convictions about truth, but who, at the same time, have great respect for people. While it may be true that "error has no rights," *people* have all sorts of rights—including the right to hold tenaciously to erroneous views. (I do not raise here the problem of whether this is an ultimate right before God. It certainly is a right of man over against his fellow men and it is so recognized wherever there is religious and civil liberty.) Sacredness of personality is the basis for a genuine tolerance of people, within a framework of quiet, shared conviction about the truth as it is in Christ.

There is no question about the nature of the apostolic witness at this point. It was dogmatically assertive of the finality of Jesus Christ. Peter spoke for all when he insisted: "Neither is there salvation in any other: for there is none other name under heaven given among men, whereby we must be saved" (Acts 4:12). Salvation in no other? How can this be?

Perhaps the best way to illustrate it is by relating an actual experience in the life of Emil Brunner, the famous Swiss theologian. In India two Hindu professors came to him and asked how Christians could say that "in none other is there salvation." They were quite willing to include Christ along with the other great bearers of salvation, but they were offended at the claim that he was the sole source of salvation. In responding, Brunner pointed out that the finality of Jesus Christ stems from the fact that he and he alone died for the sins of the world, giving his life a ransom for many. Neither Buddha nor Krishna nor Rama died for the sins of mankind. "But one thing there is not in Indian religion or in any religion outside Christianity: a man who came on earth to reconcile to God by the sacrifice of his life those who had become separated from God by their guilt and sin."[10]

What Brunner is saying here is that it is the historical character of its gospel that gives Christianity its note of exclusiveness and finality. That is what we have been pointing out throughout this chapter. It is conceivable that an

[10] From *The Great Invitation,* by Emil Brunner; trans. by Harold Knight (Philadelphia: The Westminster Press, Copyright, 1955), p. 108. Used by permission.

eternal being might reveal himself again and again through the ages, in many different ways. Indeed, biblical faith has always believed this ("God, who at sundry times and in divers manners spake in time past unto the fathers by the prophets. . . ." Heb. 1:1). But if in Jesus Christ God really did what he is said to have done, if he really broke the power of sin and death, if he really triumphed over the world, the flesh, and the devil, if he really atoned for the sin of the world, then there is a finality about this deed that cannot be gainsaid. If it has been done and done right—it is almost blasphemous to speak this way—then it has been done, period. And that's the end of it. It is unrepeatable. If what the gospel claims is *fact,* then the deed of redemption has been done once for all, constituting him who wrought it as mankind's Savior and only Lord. To serve other lords is to be idolatrous. This is the "intolerance" of the gospel, and it stems from the appeal we make to historical, objective fact.

Bishop Nygren of the Swedish church has his own way of making the point. He reminds his readers of the plight of Denmark in World War II. For long years Denmark was occupied by usurping powers; she was under the heel of the Nazi regime. Then in May, 1945, the Nazis, having been hammered relentlessly all over Europe by the Allies, withdrew to the borders of Germany. Out from the nerve centers of Denmark to the places where brave men hid in terror of their lives there went a message: "The invader has been defeated. Denmark is free." Patriots returned to their homes and families, to walk again the streets and lanes of an emancipated Denmark.[11]

The gospel is a message like that. It is the telling of

[11] Adapted from *The Gospel of God,* by Anders Nygren, trans. by L. J. Trinterud (Philadelphia: The Westminster Press, Copyright, 1951), p. 29. Used by permission.

Something That Happened at a particular time and at a particular place. It is the message of how in Jesus Christ, God decisively injected himself into our human tragedy and effected a great deliverance in which all may share who listen believingly to the message of the gospel: "The usurping powers have been defeated. Humanity is free."[12]

[12] The problem of what happens to the heathen who have never heard the gospel is discussed in Appendix A. See page 177.

2

THE CHRIST WHO WAS

WE WANT NOW TO SPELL OUT something of the meaning
of the gospel. But before we look at the good news of
Christ, we must look at the bad news of man. Indeed, what
makes the gospel such wonderful news is the appalling
human situation to which it is addressed. To this we must
now turn.

Man is fallen, man is corrupted, man is diseased, man is
lost, man is dead. These are biblical figures for describing
the plight of man. They all are efforts to say that something
has gone seriously wrong with human nature and that only
a desperate and radical solution is possible. Where is the
trouble? It lies in a failure of relationship.

Man is a peculiar creature. He can be understood only
in his relationships, and he can be understood in that way
only because that is the way in which he exists. A person is
what he is by virtue of his relations. This fact is what makes
him peculiarly human. A stone is just "there," to be noted
and analyzed. But a man is not just "there." He is a related
being, and he cannot be noted and analyzed except in and
through the relationships that make him what he is. The
basic relations—basic in the sense that they are peculiar to
man—are three: his relation to God, his relation to his
fellows, and his relation to himself.

Man is related to God as his image, as the one who is
called into being for free fellowship with God, who is his
life. He is made in and for the love of God. God addresses

41

him as his offspring, and man answers him. It is this fact which makes man a *responsible* being. He is able to respond to God. Also it is this fact which makes man human.

Furthermore, man is related to his fellows in a special way. The psychologists tell us that personality is a social concept. By this they mean that unless a child is surrounded by human beings in the give and take of social intercourse, he will not develop human characteristics. Give him animals to rear him and he will remain a subhuman. Accordingly, in a real sense my fellow human beings help to make me. They are my comakers, as it were. "I can only be myself through some personal encounter with you, and to that encounter I do not bring a ready-made self; I grow into a self as I share life from moment by moment with you and other selves."[1] How easily the character of others influences my own!

Finally, man is related to himself in a most surprising manner. He can carry on a dialogue with himself. "I" can talk to "me." I can accuse myself, or excuse myself, or justify myself to myself. I can have a good image of "me" or a bad one, a right idea of who I am basically or a wrong one. But more, I can do things with "me." By the decisions that I make, I—along with God and my fellows—help to create "me" along the lines that I desire.

This ability to create, with which man is endowed, is part of the image of God in man. God is the Creator, with a capital C. But when God willed to make man in his own likeness, he willed to give him a limited, finite creativity. Man's creativity expresses itself in his creation of culture, as well as in his ability to shape and mold himself.

Man makes tools and produces goods by means of them.

[1] From *The Self and Its Hazards: A Guide to the Thought of Karl Jaspers,* by E. L. Allen (London: Hodder and Stoughton, Ltd., n.d.), p. 25. Used by permission.

Through music, painting, and literature, he creates beauty in the likeness of the God who has given us sunsets, flowers, and landscapes. Through law and government, man takes a hand in shaping behavior and encouraging right conduct. Through the voluntary associations of society, man creates structures and organizations which promote human fellowship and service to one's neighbor.

But man's creativity is most spectacularly seen in his ability to form and fashion himself. A man is a creation of God left unfinished purposely by his Creator so that man might have the privilege of finishing himself by his own free choices. That he can do this is man's glory. He is at one and the same time the craftsman who does the fashioning and the raw material on which the work is done.

But if man's ability to have a hand in his own character and destiny is man's glory, it is also his shame, for he has made a miserable mess of it. History is the story of how he has done this. Briefly, man's God-given ability went to his head. He forgot that he was intended to live as a child before his heavenly Father; he wanted to be an adult—to be on his own. He forgot that he was intended to be God's junior partner in creativity; he wanted to form his own corporation and go into business for himself. He forgot that, although given a share in the divine creativity, he was after all only a creature; he wanted to be the Creator, the maker of heaven and earth. His success as a limited and finite creator of sorts depended completely on his staying close enough to the Master Craftsman to follow his pattern and his way of doing things. After all, it was God who had structured the universe—including man—to function in a certain way. When man refused to be confined to the divine plan and purpose and "turned . . . to his own way" (Isa. 53:6), only catastrophe could follow—and it did! Instead of man's creativity being constructive, it became destructive

and even demonic. Man's institutions became infected with
evil. They became monuments to his foolishness and pride,
instead of instruments of his constructive creativity. Or they
became both at one and the same time.

In all of this a final irony crowns man's folly. Being himself, along with his civilizations, the product of a creativity-
gone-wrong, he confirms his perverted creativity by making
his God in his own image! The diverse and contradictory
religions of mankind are the most tragic result of man's
creativity-gone-wrong. Gods many and lords many strew
the landscape of history. Sinful man feels that no great help
is needed from the side of the Divine by way of revelation;
at a moment's opportunity, he will tell you all about God
and religion. He knows just who God is and what God is
like ("He's too good to damn a man"); he knows just what
God requires ("I pay my debts and mind my own business,
that's enough"); and he knows just how God will react
("We're all going to the same place"). The religions of
the world emerge when the truth of God is filtered through
the distorting medium of man's sinful and defiant spirit.

We have found it necessary to use the word "sinful."
Now, sin has been defined in many ways: as the desire for
your own way, as estrangement from God, as man's effort
to play the role of God to himself, as self-love, as man's
attempt to overstep the bounds of his creaturehood, as breaking the divine law, and as falling short of Christlikeness. I
think all of these are true insights. My own preference for
a short, easily-understood definition of sin is "self-suffi-
ciency." Everybody knows what that means. But however
one defines sin, sin is our problem.

It is *sin* in our lives that we are talking about, not *sins*.
Tillich has suggested that we should never use the plural
term. He may be right, it is so misleading. When we speak
of sins we become moralistic and start to analyze what are

right acts and what are wrong acts. Now there *are* right acts and there *are* wrong acts. But these are not what we are talking about when we speak of sin. Here we are not concerned so much with what people *do* as with what they *are*. To put it another way, we are not concerned so much with what people do as with what their relationships are. Sin is the spoiling of relationships. It is basically the spoiling of our relation to God (if there were no God there would be no sin), but our relation to our fellows and to ourselves is radically affected also. Sin acquires a different quality according to whether we think of the disruption of our God-relation, neighbor-relation, or self-relation. Suppose we spell this out.

Sin, seen from the perspective of our Godward relation, means guilt. Of course it does. Sin is man's refusal to let God function as God in his life. Hence it is an effort on man's part to usurp God's place, to nudge God off his throne, to set up a human will against the divine will, to live as though there were no God, or at least as though it were a minor matter whether or not there is a God. The man who does this is guilty. He is guilty of breaking the divine law, of defying his Creator, of high treason against Heaven, of refusing to assume his assigned place in the scheme of things, call-it-what-you-will.

Sin in relation to our fellows means lovelessness. Of course it does. In the plan of God, the love of God is the cement that holds society together. As the conductor of an orchestra brings order out of chaos by co-ordinating and organizing the individual efforts of the musicians through loyalty and obedience to himself, so God serves as the co-ordinator and organizer of society. Each man, in loyalty to the God who made him, takes his assigned place in the social structure and makes his assigned contribution to the common good. God is loved by all, his love is in all and

through all, and in God each man is rightly related in love
to his neighbor. This is the ideal. But when God is nudged
aside and each man wants his own way instead of God's
way, society falls apart into warring and competitive groups
and individuals. The common co-ordinator is lacking. Each
man is on his own to carve out his own niche, to find his
own friends, and to make his own life. No common overarching truth or loyalty holds men together. Severed from
the love of God, they are unable to grasp the world of other
persons in genuine neighbor-love. Each tends to make himself, with his ideas, plans, desires, and viewpoints, the center
of the universe. The common center has gone.

Sin in relation to my own self-relation means perversion
and bondage. Naturally, I am so constructed that I can
function properly only when God is the center of my life,
and when, within this center, my neighbor also finds a place
in my life. God, neighbor, and I are all bound up in a
common life and love. God created me to be open, as it
were, on all sides of me—embracing in my life and being
both God and my neighbor. But now sin enters. I am
severed from the life and love of God, my neighbor slips
away from me, and I find a new center in—myself. I, who
was made to be open, am now shut down tight over myself,
egocentric. With God lost, I am thrown back on myself to
live off my own nerves and feed off my own fingernails, to
live by my own wits and fuss over my own anxieties. Obviously the "I" talked about here is quite a different "I" from
the "I" that is open in love to God and neighbor. This
sinful "I" is all tangled up in itself, twisted in on itself in
grotesque distortion of what it was made to be. Severed
from the elemental energies of life, cut off from the source
of its good, alienated from the God who made it for life in
God, this arrogantly independent "I" has lost its true nature
but must keep on existing. Hence it invents new forms and

channels of expression—all of which expose its essential unnaturalness and malfunctioning. The self has lost the ability to be what it was made to be.

So there we have it. Man as sinner is guilty, loveless, and unfree (perverted). When we say that man is loveless, we do not mean that he is incapable of ever loving anyone or of ever doing a sacrificial act. We mean that his basic posture over against the rest of humanity (not just his friends, but humanity itself) is not one of outgoing love and concern. He does not love his neighbor as himself, and we must remember that the term "neighbor" as Jesus used it is not a matter of geography but of need. Since man is guilty, loveless, and unfree, any redemption that is offered to him must address itself to his situation at these three points.[2]

It is of some interest that modern psychiatry deals with these same three problems: the problem of guilt, the problem of the inability to give and receive love, and the problem of the lack of freedom to function properly. This parallel concern of Christianity and psychiatry with man's guilt-feelings, his lovelessness, and his unfreedom, has raised interesting questions as to the relation between the two. The relation appears to be both positive and negative. On the one hand, we should rejoice in all that psychiatry teaches us about man and all that it does for man. But psychiatry is not the gospel. The psychiatrist may remove neurotic guilt, but there still remains realistic guilt—and only God can take that away. A psychiatrist may help a loveless neurotic to give and receive love on the human level, but only God himself can renew him in the *agapē* love of God. A psychiatrist

_____

[2] Many of the things mentioned in this chapter are discussed from a somewhat different though similar approach in my small book, *The Price and the Prize* (Philadelphia: The Judson Press, 1953). It is my hope that what was said there and what is said here supplement each other. But some might find the discussion in that book the more illuminating.

may release a man from the neurotic unfreedom that makes it impossible for him to function as a useful member of his society, but only God can give to him the liberty of the sons of God, the liberty which makes it possible for him to function as a useful member of the divine society, the community of believers. In short, psychiatry and the gospel work at man's problems on different though not unrelated levels. The well-integrated, well-adjusted, and socially well-manicured person still needs redemption. Still, the fact that psychiatry has developed parallel concerns shows how very modern the gospel is in its analysis of man's need.

But back to the gospel of redemption. Since sin is disruption of relationships, salvation can only be restoration of relationships. It is not a mere going to heaven when you die; it is something more basic, of which going to heaven at death is a consequence. In one word, it is reconciliation. Salvation or redemption (I am using the terms interchangeably, though some theologians make a distinction) is a matter of reconciliation: with God, with one's neighbor, and with one's true self. No one can hope for salvation who is not willing to be right with God, his neighbor, and himself. It is important to note this, for while many people would be delighted to be saved from the *consequences* of their sin while their essential self remained untouched, there are far fewer who are willing to see themselves torn apart and put together again by divine grace. Probably most people dodge the encounter with Christ precisely because they are afraid it will make too great a change in their lives. Having put so much time and energy into making ourselves what we are, we hate to admit that it all has been a mistake and that we need radical alteration. We have developed an overwhelming stake in the status quo. The self that we are is the only self we are acquainted with, and we fear that surrendering this to the Master Craftsman for alteration might result in the loss of our identity. That is why either a great dissatisfaction with ourselves or a great impression of the love of God or both is preliminary to a commitment to Christ.

What the gospel promises, then, is reconciliation. But here there is a surprise. The reconciler is not man the sinner, but God the sinned against. He does the reconciling; this is the good news. It is not that man has found a way to God, but rather that God has found a way to man. No other religion, only Christianity, has dared to affirm that the reconciler is God himself. "God was in Christ, reconciling the world unto himself" (2 Cor. 5:19).

Redemption as Forgiveness

We have seen that in relation to God, sin means guilt. Instead of being Father, God stands as Judge. Instead of being the trusted One, he becomes the suspected One. Instead of being the One sought, he becomes the One avoided. Guilt drives a breach between man and God. What, then, does it mean to be redeemed at this point? It means to be brought into fellowship with God through his freely offered pardon in Jesus Christ. "In whom we have redemption through his blood, the forgiveness of our sins" (Eph. 1:7). Redemption is—forgiveness. "Forgiveness without reason matched sin without excuse."

Now, the idea that God freely forgives us in Christ has been attacked on two grounds. Christian forgiveness is attacked, on the one hand, as too easy; on the other, as too hard. Obviously, this needs some explaining.

Those who object to the realities of Christian forgiveness as too *easy* do so on the basis of its clash with justice. As a university student once said to me: "Forgiveness is an immoral solution to the problem of wrongdoing. A man ought to make restitution for his sins." A distinguished contemporary philosopher is reported to have said that he could not respect a God who forgave. More will be said about this shortly, but two preliminary remarks are in order.

First, forgiveness is not unknown between human beings, and when it takes place it usually is acclaimed as a wonderful and noble thing. One has the suspicion that to these detractors the idea of forgiveness is horrifying only on the divine level; on the human level, it is quite praiseworthy. If true, one can hazard a guess as to why it is true. Forgiveness is a terribly humiliating thing to accept, and the idea that a man can do nothing for his own salvation except to sue for pardon strikes an intolerable blow at a man's pride. The second preliminary remark that is in order is this: the idea of forgiveness as immoral, while true of some kinds of forgiveness, is a misunderstanding of the Christian meaning of that term. To this also we shall return later.

Those who attack the Christian idea of forgiveness as too *hard* appeal to the uselessness of the cross. They say: "Why must forgiveness come to me through this horror? If there be a loving God, let him forgive and have done with it. Why all this mummery about blood and a cross and a man dying in torture? Surely we have the right to infer that if a man repents, God will pardon."

The quickest answer to this group is to confront them with the arguments of the first group, namely, that forgiveness is an immoral concept. The two kinds of objections cancel each other out. The first group think Christians make forgiveness too simple; the second group think they make it too complex. It is clear, therefore, that the word "forgiveness," as Christians use it, needs some looking into.

First of all, if God is to forgive, his forgiveness must operate in such a way that the moral structure of the universe is not impaired, but rather is upheld. This means that forgiveness must never be interpreted as condoning evil or acting as though its existence really did not make any difference. It is a fact that a too-cheap forgiveness can ruin the character of the one forgiven, and if practiced on a wide enough scale can undermine the stability of the society which permits its citizens to "get away with it." Every parent is familiar with this problem. If a child gets the impression that forgiveness is simple, a mere matter on his part of saying, "I'm sorry," and getting in return a pardoning pat on the head, the seriousness of wrongdoing is removed. Easygoing parental indulgence teaches the child to trade on his parents' good nature. The teen-age boy of one of my professors ended up behind prison bars, damned by the cheap forgiveness of an indulgent parent.

The social side of this is equally clear. A society which lacks concern for law and justice and for the punishment that stems from such concern is headed for disaster. There is a good deal of confusion here in people's thinking. Punishment need not be vindictive, nor need it be contrary to an interest in the welfare of the criminal and in his rehabilitation. Indeed, it may be an element *in* his rehabilitation.

This leads me to a second comment about forgiveness— a comment that is related to the first comment, yet is not exactly the same. Forgiveness, to be morally effective, must satisfy the conscience and moral sense of the one forgiven. In recent years we have learned from the psychologists a lot about repressed guilt. Many people who do not consciously have guilt feelings do so unconsciously. Indeed, Freud said that all of us have some elements of guilt-feelings buried down in the cellars of our personalities, down in the unconscious. Such guilt feelings seek expiation and people have various ways of punishing themselves for unconscious guilt: through sickness, or proneness to accidents, or proneness to failure in life, etc. Some criminals will—unconsciously—leave clues so they will get caught and be punished. Some people are so torn apart by guilt feelings that their personalities disintegrate and they end up in mental hospitals.

Although much guilt-feeling is neurotic, much is realistic; and even here there can appear a genuine need for being punished. Forgiveness must be offered in such a way and within such a context that guilt-feelings are not ignored, by-passed, or overlaid, but actually dealt with.

A third comment seems necessary at this point—again related to what we already have said, but not quite the same. If forgiveness is to avoid the charge of "immoral," it must be something more than a means of escaping the consequences of sin. It surely is clear that it would be quite intolerable if the only result of forgiveness were to wipe out an accumulation of debts, leaving the sinner free to return to the same old sinful life and the same old sinful ways—only to seek forgiveness again, have it granted, and go back once more to the same old life and the same old ways; and so on indefinitely.

Finally, forgiveness must be offered in such a way that the forgiven one is not humiliated and his self-respect is not taken away. We all are familiar with the "selfless" mother-type who "gives her all" for her child—and never lets the child forget it. Such a mother can scar a child deeply by constant reminders of her "self-sacrifice" and constant innuendoes of ingratitude. Less obnoxious, but still objectionable, is the person who is always "doing" for her friends, but who will not let her friends do anything in return. She wants to be in no one's debt, while keeping everyone in hers.

Now just as self-sacrifice and generosity can be perverse and perverted, so also can forgiveness. Forgiveness—which ideally should always stem from love—can stem from less noble motives. It may arise from the need to feel virtuous, at the expense of the one forgiven; or to feel superior, which is worse. A person even can forgive another from contempt: the erring one is really not worth getting upset about; he and all that he does is so unworthy of my notice that I refuse to get excited and would rather shrug off the whole thing by contemptuously "forgiving" the offender.

It is clear that any form of forgiveness that arises from self-righteousness, or arrogance, or contempt, or that serves to make a public spectacle or "horrible example" of the one pardoned can only humiliate the wrongdoer.

I can illustrate the need of forgiving in the right way, that is to say, in a way that preserves the self-respect of the offender, by relating an episode in the life of Dr. Gordon Brownville. I once used in a little leaflet a story I had heard him tell. It was the story of how, as a boy, he had been involved in taking without permission a neighbor's automobile, only to have the automobile stolen while left unattended. The neighbor insisted on having him arrested. The climax of the story was his father's hurried return from an out-of-town trip with his quiet word of forgiveness to a boy already overwhelmed with shame and guilt.

This was the climax of the story as I told it. But the leaflet fell into Dr. Brownville's hands. He wrote me to add a postscript: his father had never mentioned the episode again. To me, the point of the story was the forgiveness. But to the person pardoned, the point of the story was the *manner* of the forgiveness. It was a healing and not a wounding form of pardon.

These four things, then, must be true of any forgiveness

worthy of the name.[3] Let us now see how the gospel measures up in the light of them.

1. The gospel safeguards the moral structure of the universe. This is precisely the significance of the cross. This safeguarding is done in several ways. For one way, the cross teaches us that we should not *assume* forgiveness. We have seen that some objectors to the gospel do make this assumption. That is why they feel the cross is unnecessary. "We have the right," they say, "to assume that God will forgive us if we repent." But there is danger in this position, a danger highlighted by those who carry it one step further and derive forgiveness from God—by definition. "God will forgive," said Voltaire. "It is his business to forgive." Such an attitude obviously takes away all seriousness from sin. In the gospel, on the other hand, forgiveness is neither inferred nor derived by definition from the nature of God. It is declared as a matter of revelation—and offered to all men freely by God who effected it at such tremendous cost.

At the core of the revelation of forgiveness is the disclosure of the terrible price that God must pay in order to forgive. Forgiveness is not a cheap and easy thing, if the cross be true. Rather it is infinitely painful and terribly costly. It may be offered to the sinner freely; such is the divine love. But it is hammered out of the heartbreak and agony of God himself. The One who forgives is the One who suffers. He lures the guilt of an alienated race to his own heart, and lets that guilt break it. Then, when from the cross the divine words of forgiveness are uttered, the words

[3] Those who have read Stephen Neill's *Christian Faith Today* will recognize my indebtedness to him in this discussion. Those who have not read Neill should do so. To encourage them in the effort, let me mention that *Christian Faith Today* is available in the Penguin series, paper back, for 65 cents. Another excellent and readable book on the gospel, with special reference to forgiveness, is James Stewart's *A Faith to Proclaim* (Charles Scribner's Sons, 1953). The interested, intelligent layman should be able to read with profit both of these books. Stewart's is the easier.

are wrapped in tragedy, reflecting the wounds endured by God himself, the Reconciler.

The cross is the proclamation of the righteousness of God and of his judgment on sin. The cross makes forgiveness possible without making righteousness secondary. This is what P. T. Forsyth is saying when he writes:

> God's love is the love for sinners of a God above all things holy, whose holiness makes sin damnable as sin and love active as grace. It can only act in a way that shall do justice to holiness, and restore it. Short of that, love does no more than pass a lenient sentence on sin. It meets the strain of the situation by reducing the severity of the demands.[4]

And a little later, speaking of Christ's entering "the dark shadow of God's penalty on sin," he adds: "to forgive sin he must bear sin"; "to bear holy love to us he must bear holy wrath for us." Forgiveness is thus invested with a firm moral quality.

In the light of the cross there can be no easy trading on God's good nature. When a man understands the cost of forgiveness, he cannot go out and sin lightly again. Christian forgiveness may seem "immoral" to some objectors, but historically it has proved quite the opposite. It has produced in millions of lives a new concern for righteousness and a new life of holiness. It is not too much to say with James Stewart that the gospel of forgiveness has proved the mightiest force for righteousness in the world. The gratitude released by this gospel—again connected with the pardoned sinner's understanding of the cost of it—has seen to that.

2. The gospel deals with the conscience and moral sensibilities of the sinner. Here again we appeal to the cross. The cross does not by-pass the sinner's sense of guilt, nor deal with it lightly in the forgiving process. It does not try

[4] From *Positive Preaching and the Modern Mind,* by P. T. Forsyth (New York: Harper and Brothers, Copyright, 1907), p. 353. Used by permission.

to ease his bad conscience by assuring him that there is nothing to get excited about, for it is a small matter after all and can be taken care of quite easily and simply. On the contrary, the cross assures the guilt-ridden man that his guilt-feelings are grounded in reality, and that his bad conscience is not to be deadened by soporifics or pep talks.[5] Also it assures him of something else. There is a solution to his guiltiness. Here Brunner speaks eloquently:

> Can our guilt be just annihilated? Is there not in it an ultimate reality? Yes indeed, says the cross of Christ, your guilt *is* an ultimate reality so that not even the love of God can simply pass it by. The suffering which you feel that your guilt ought to inflict upon you has been supremely suffered in Him in whom God gives you forgiveness and love. God takes your guilt so seriously that He takes it upon Himself.[6]

3. The forgiveness offered in the gospel is no mere escape from the consequences of our sin. Indeed, it is clear that some things which we do have consequences which *cannot* be dodged, even though we may be forgiven (e.g., the fathering of an illegitimate child). But the whole discussion of forgiveness in terms of escaping consequences is a misunderstanding of the main point of Christian forgiveness. Christian forgiveness is more than a declaration of pardon. It is the establishment of intimate and life-renewing fellowship with the God who pardons. In forgiving us, God gathers us into his continuing love and care. Right relations are forged between God and us in and through which the pardoned sinner is reborn. In the Christian faith there is no such thing

[5] I have to assume the good sense of my reader here. It is impossible to go into all the problems of guilt and personality, especially emotionally sick personalities. I am not unaware of some situations where people *do* need reassurance against an overactive and oversensitive conscience. I am only trying to make here one small, limited point, which I hope will not be lost in digressions about clinical psychology and counseling techniques.

[6] From *Faith, Hope and Love*, by Emil Brunner (Philadelphia: The Westminster Press, Copyright, 1956), p. 29. Used by permission.

as a mere forgiveness which sends the unchanged sinner back to live his old life. There is more to God's pardon than rubbing black marks off a man's record. There is cleansing and renewal and a new life in union with Christ. That is why Forsyth can speak of the effectual character of God's forgiveness in Christ. It is effectual precisely because it operates, "not by way of amnesty, not by way of mere pardon, not by way of mere mercy upon our repentance, but by the radical way of redemption."[7] Redemption is forgiveness plus.

4. The forgiveness of which the gospel speaks does not humiliate the recipient; it releases him. True, the gospel, at the beginning of God's encounter with us, is like a steam roller. It is calculated to crush the self that we are. As Kierkegaard explains it, Christianity is God pounding the table before us; and God can pound awfully hard. But the crushing is not an end in itself, but a means to an end. God seeks to crush the self-that-is that the self-that-might-be may be born, and born in all its God-given dignity. The forgiven self is not abased and overwhelmed, but is given a new self-respect by virtue of the fact that God wills fellowship with it. This restoration to fellowship is the inward meaning and intent of God's pardoning grace in Christ.

There is an episode in Marjorie Kinnan Rawlings' book, *The Yearling,* which is dear to the heart of every illustration-loving preacher. The boy, Jody, is told that he must destroy his beloved fawn, Flag, because of widespread damage to the farm. Jody obeys; but he tells his father that he hates him, and then, thinking that after that there is no place for him anymore in the family, he runs away from home. After a few days his hunger, fatigue and loneliness forces him to crawl back home. He is astonished to find that his disappearance had completely disrupted the home

[7] P. T. Forsyth, *op. cit.,* p. 366.

and almost killed his grieving father. Jody could not get over it. It was unbelievable, but true. He was wanted, actually *wanted!*

Our Lord tells the same story in the parable of the prodigal son. It is the glory of the gospel that it tells of a God who, after all that can be said of his majesty and holiness and omnipotence and all else, so wants the erring, guilty, hostile sinner that he follows him into the darkness and to the ultimate issue, the agony of the cross, that he may win him back to hearth and home. God does not wait for us to show up; the initiative is his. Then, when God finds us, he comes "not as one who confers a favor out of his superfluity; He comes asking a favor of us. He stands as a beggar at our door; He makes no effort to break in upon our independence; He merely pleads that we will be so good as not to refuse the gift which He has traveled so far to bring."[8] By God's grace we can walk into the future untainted by the past. Wanted though unworthy. "Accepted though unacceptable." What grace!

Redemption as Wholeness

If forgiveness is God's answer to sin as guilt, wholeness is his answer for sin as perversion. Salvation is wholeness. This is brought out by comparing Luke 7:50 with Luke 8:48. In Luke 7:50 Jesus says to the forgiven woman, "Thy faith hath saved thee; go in peace." In the next chapter he says to the healed woman (8:48), "Thy faith hath made thee whole; go in peace." But in the original Greek, exactly the same verb is used in both verses. To be saved *is* to be made whole. This usage of the verb "to save" (or the noun "salvation," though Christ is recorded as having used the noun only twice) is the usual one on the lips of our

[8] From *Christian Faith Today,* by Stephen Neill (Baltimore, Penguin Books, Copyright, 1955), p. 160. Used by permission.

Lord. Sometimes he speaks in terms of physical healing; sometimes in terms of moral and spiritual change. But the general meaning of the word is the same in all cases.

Salvation is a power that comes to a man from beyond him to remake him. It is the counteracting of destructive forces and the restoration to men of what they have lost through them. On the physical level, this is well illustrated by the story of the healing of the man with the withered hand (Mark 3:1-6). Christ asked the complainers whether it was lawful on the sabbath to save life or to destroy it. When he made the withered hand as good as new, it was clear what he had in mind by the phrase, "to save life." It was the arresting of the forces which bound the man for evil and the restoration of his perverted members to proper and normal functioning. So when Christ says that his mission is to seek and to save that which is lost (Luke 19: 10)—the statement follows immediately on his pronouncement that salvation has come to Zacchaeus, as proved by the fact that he is now functioning as a son of Abraham and child of God *should* function (Luke 19:8-9)—this is precisely what is meant. The Savior of men seeks out those destructive forces that wither and pervert life that he may destroy them and restore their victims to normal life. Salvation is the power to be our true selves in the freedom wrought by Christ. Redemption is more than forgiveness for guilt; it is the correction of a disability and the consequent release into the liberty of true manhood.

It is illuminating to look into some of the bondages from which Christ frees a man. There is, of course, the bondage of sin. As Paul refers to it in the discussion in Romans 6:20 and following, he makes a point pertinent to any discussion of freedom. There is no such thing as freedom in the abstract. All freedom is *from* something *to* something. In a very real sense, we are released from one bondage to assume the yoke of another. The mind can be in bondage to error and free of truth, or it can be in bondage to truth and free of error. It cannot just be free, period. But—and here is the paradox—bondage to error is really bondage, whereas bondage to truth is really freedom! The mind is *made* for truth, and its liberty is to be able to function in the way for which it was made, i.e., to be bound to the truth. Perhaps we can see this even more clearly in relation to physical health and disease. You can be in bondage to the laws of health or in bondage to the power of disease. But there is a tremendous difference. Bondage to disease is real bondage, whereas bondage to health is really freedom. Why? We were made for health; disease is an alien power. To be in bondage to health and its laws is to be free to function in the way for which we were made physically.

This is the point that Paul is constantly emphasizing in his epistles. In Romans 6 (the whole chapter merits study) he refers to the bondage of sin. In other places he refers to the bondage of the flesh. Romans 8:4 and following is an example. There "flesh" has its usual meaning in Paul's writings. It is used as a synonym of unredeemed, natural man, *not* as a synonym for body. But the meaning is the same as that in Romans 6. A man can be in bondage either to sin or to God. But bondage to sin is real, genuine bondage, issuing in perversion and death; whereas bondage to God is freedom. For we were made for God and can only function normally in right relations with him. This is wholeness, i.e., holiness (which is right character, as righteousness is right conduct), and is the gift of God's grace in his Son, Jesus Christ. To be made free from sin by Christ does not mean that we shall never commit a sin again. It does mean that sin shall not be our master.[9]

Now, when in Christ we are free from the bondage of

[9] We will return to this matter in Chapter 4.

sin, we are at the same time free from the fetters of ignorance (Eph. 4:17-24). The ignorance from which we are freed is not the ignorance of information which can be learned from books. It is the ignorance of who we are, why we are here, and what we ought to do. In Christ we know the truth, and it makes us free. Such freedom releases a man from the bondage of meaninglessness, for it gives direction and purpose to his life.

Further, to be free in the liberty of the sons of God is to be free from fear. Fear can take many forms, all of them enslaving. For instance, there can be fear of the future. This fear can either paralyze into inactivity or spur to overactivity for the sake of security. How prevalent the fear of the unknown future is, we all can testify. Redemption releases a man from this bondage by drawing him into the circle of God's overarching care. "Take therefore no thought (i.e., don't be fretful) for the tomorrow," our Lord teaches (Matt. 6:34 and preceding). "In nothing be anxious," Paul exhorts (Phil. 4:6, ASV). "Cast all your anxieties on him, for he cares about you," Peter pleads (1 Pet. 5:7, RSV).

Another fear from which we are offered release in the gospel is the fear of men. This truth is written on every page of the Book of Acts. In John 20:19, we find the disciples meeting behind closed doors for fear of their enemies. But after Pentecost, they were released from the fear of being themselves and of expressing themselves fully in the liberty of Christ. They were fearless, because they were committed men—committed for time and eternity to the purposes of a loving Savior, in whose hands their destiny lay. We today have seen the power of the gospel to create truly free men. It is a fact worth pondering that the main resistance to totalitarian evil has come, not from the universities, not from the corporations, and not from the trade unions, but from the churches. Those who have been bought with a price can never be the slaves of men. The Niemöllers, the Bergraavs, the Verniers and all the nameless heroes who share their fearless faith, cannot prostrate themselves before government because they have already prostrated themselves before God. They cannot be broken by men, because they have already been broken by Christ. They cannot be tempted by promises of safety and security, because they already have safety and security in the Love which will not let them go.

There is an important corollary to our release in Christ from the fear of men. Hate comes from fear, and when we no longer fear what men can do to us, we need no longer hate them. This is important for the peace of the world.

Likewise there is a fear of *God* from which we are set free in Christ. Of course, there is a fear of God which is right and wise. We speak with approval of a "God-fearing man," and quote Scripture to the effect that "the fear of the Lord is the beginning of wisdom." But there is also an enslaving fear of God, born of hostility and alienation and accentuated by guilt. It is this fear from which we are freed in Christ. "Herein is our love made perfect, that we may have boldness in the day of judgment. . . . There is no fear in love; but perfect love casteth out fear: because fear hath torment" (1 John 4:17-18).

But before the day of judgment comes death—our final fear. All creatures die; but only man knows that he must die and lives his life in that knowledge.

> "Nor dread nor hope attend
> a dying animal;
> A man awaits his end
> Dreading and hoping all;
>
> *   *   *
>
> He knows death to the bone—
> Man has created death.[10]

[10] W. B. Yeats, "Death."

But Christ is stronger even than death. Christ, through his self-sacrifice, has delivered those "who through fear of death were all their lifetime subject to bondage" (Heb. 2:15).

Let us do a little summarizing here. The redemption of Christ is a redemption to liberty, true liberty. Because of Christ, we are able to *be,* in the real sense of that word. He is the Great Deliverer who frees us from every bondage that reduces the fullness of life. Because of him the tyrannies of life are broken and we are freed from the fetters of sin, ignorance, meaninglessness, and fear—fear of the future, fear of men, fear of death, and fear of God.

This list is hardly exhaustive, but rather suggestive. But there is one other slavery which is ended in Christ which merits mention here, because reference to it leads so easily into the next section. I refer to the constricting influence of the world upon the life and character of the individual. "Love not the world," exhorts the Apostle John (1 John 2:15). "Be not conformed to this world," writes the Apostle Paul (Romans 12:2—using the Greek word for "age"). What is at stake here is nothing less than a man's right to be a real person, independently of the pressures toward conformity from those who share his time and place with him. Man's social environment is the world, with all of its standards, ideals of success, and institutions, organized without reference to the will of God (though not necessarily uninfluenced by the Christians who live in it). The pressure of the social environment upon the individual is immense, even though he often is unconscious of it. We tend to see things through American, white, middle-class eyes. It is hard to transcend our culture. But it is not impossible. When the liberating grace of Jesus Christ touches a man he is no longer a tumbling tumbleweed, blown helplessly about by every wind of influence. He is no little Sir Echo who merely repeats the slogans and phrases of his age. He has been given a citizenship in a new kingdom, the kingdom of God, and he is no longer bound to the mores, customs, prejudices, and viewpoints of the world. He is no longer *bound*. That is to say, he may acquiesce in certain mores and customs insofar as he finds them good and healthy. But he is discriminating, able to accept or reject, because he sees now through the eyes of Christ.

It is tempting to pause here and explore at somewhat greater length the meaning of the wordliness from which we are delivered in Christ. The temptation arises from the fact that large segments of our more orthodox churches have narrowed the idea of wordliness down to certain kinds of amusements. There are indeed forms of pleasure that have upon them the mark of this world and are not of Christ. But the attitudes of worldliness are far more pervasive and subtle than these, as an old, old story illustrates. The demons of the second echelon had tried to tempt a saintly hermit of the early Christian centuries to sin, and they had failed miserably. But when Satan himself took a hand in it, the results were different. He merely whispered in the hermit's ear, "Have you heard that your brother was made Bishop of Alexandria yesterday?" A rush of jealousy flooded the hermit's soul. This, too, is worldliness.

Again, the temptations of our Lord in the wilderness were temptations to conform to the methods of this world in launching his ministry. In the end, he who had been from the beginning crucified *to* the world (the phrase, of course, is Paul's) was crucified *by* it.

Paul makes more than passing reference to the "world" as it reveals itself and is embedded in the social structures of his day: master-slave relations, husband-wife relations, parent-child relations, and government-citizen (or subject) relations. All of these are, in the last analysis, superior-inferior relations. I do not mean that a wife is *really* inferior to her husband or that a citizen is *really* inferior to his ruler. Superiority and inferiority here refer to function, not character or ability.

But the point is that these relations become the occasion of sin, and even the expression of sin, because they inflate the ego on the one hand and distort the personality of the inferior on the other. They minister to the pride and ego-satisfaction of the superior, who assumes that he has arrived where he is because he deserves it. At the same time, they minister to the hostility or loss of the sense of dignity of the inferior. The one "adjusts" by assuming a condescending or authoritarian air to his inferior; the latter in turn relates himself to the person in power by either resentment and a desire to reverse roles on the one hand, or flattery, self-abasement, or fear on the other. On both of them, the spirit of this world is operating. Both the one in authority and the one subject to it are impressed by status and power over another. True interpersonal relations suffer. The social structures which embody these superior-inferior relations have become obstacles to the service of others, instead of means to such service. The spirit of the world pervades them through and through.

It is instructive to see how Paul handles this many-sided problem. He does not attack the social structure itself, but undermines its power from within. He makes the antagonists—the superior one and the inferior one alike—indifferent to the success (or lack of it), status (or lack of it), exercise of authority (or lack of it), which the relations signify. Thereby each can grasp the other in Christian brotherhood and service. The official functions remain—of father, husband, master, ruler—but their *meaning* is completely changed. They are to be no longer status-symbols for the Christian, but means for serving the other person.

The other person, no longer obsessed by his inferiority and lowliness of station, becomes in his turn free to serve the "stronger" precisely through the "inferior" position which once galled him so or made him feel unsuccessful and of no account in the world. The *meaning* of the social relations has been altered; the attitudes of the persons caught in these social relations have been changed. The institutions themselves are untouched, but their power to blight human life trapped in them (whether the life of the superior through pride or the life of the inferior through resentment or self-debasement) has gone. The fetters are broken. We are not made or marred by circumstance. The ties that bind us to our social environment have been emptied of the spirit of the world and filled with the spirit of the kingdom of God.

It is important to note briefly why Paul took this line of approach. It is especially significant in the light of the Communist revolution of our day. If the social structures are broken and recast by those who are inflamed by them because they are its victims, then nothing has really been gained. If politically we "throw the rascals out" so *we* can enjoy the fruits of rulership, then we have but substituted one group of selfish men for another. If wives gain their "freedom" just to prove that no husband can tell *them* anything, the amount of love in the world has not increased one whit. If slaves revolt against their masters because they are embittered and envious, the spirit of the world has not abated one iota. But if a person becomes emancipated from the world's jockeying for riches, position, power, and prestige, and asks only for opportunity to serve God and his fellows, wherever that opportunity may be found, then a free soul has been let loose in the world and the kingdom of God draws near. It does not make any difference whether such a one is a husband or a wife, a parent or a teen-ager, a ruler or one governed, a businessman or a laboring man. He is free. Christ died to make him so.

A second reason why Paul put his emphasis on changing the worldly attitudes rather than the institutions themselves is because most of the social structures with which he dealt were necessary in any case. Government, family life, and so forth, are not evils in and of themselves, to be done away with or rejected now that Christianity has appeared on the scene. They are necessary parts of social life, though not necessarily in the form in which they are found in any given country.

This leads to a third comment on Paul's approach. The people who are best fitted to change the customs and rules under which social order is maintained are those who have been emancipated from a *personal* involvement in the matter and are thus able to see clear-eyed and objectively. They transcend the partisan aspects of the struggle because their "citizenship is in heaven" (Phil. 3:21). They may be such a despised, disfranchised minority—as was the church in the early days—that they cannot directly address themselves to altering the massive social structures of their day; but in their own lives and fellowship, they can rise above these structures and "hold the line" for future generations. I cannot help adding that it would be nice to see a little "rising above" the American scene on the part of American Christians who are so obviously Americans first—with all their scrambling for success, immersion in the American way of life, pride of race, and nation—and Christians afterward.

To return to Paul for one final comment—the problem as to whether or not there are some social customs and institutions (like slavery) which are inherently wrong and which should be spurned by Christians must await another chapter.

Redemption as Renewal in and for Love

If for guilt God offers forgiveness, and for perversion wholeness, for lovelessness he offers love. The love of God is shed abroad in our hearts through the Holy Spirit (cf. Rom. 5:5), and we are set free from our sin and bondage— to love. "For, brethren, ye have been called unto liberty; only use not liberty for an occasion to the flesh, but by love serve one another" (Gal. 5:13). It is exceedingly important that we see what is meant here. All of what God does *in* us and *for* us is in order that he may do things *through* us for the sake of our fellowmen. Because God has no needs of his own, he has given us our neighbor to love in his stead and for his sake.

When Jesus summarized the "law and the prophets" (i.e., the Old Testament), he did so in the two great commandments: love God and love your neighbor (Matt. 22:37-40). This is Christian spirituality and maturity. The Christian faith, ultimately and finally, is concerned with right interpersonal relations, and right interpersonal relations are those in which love reigns.

To see love as the fulfilling of the law in its inner meaning and intent is to simplify things greatly. Paul lists the great commandments against adultery, killing, stealing, bearing false witness, and coveting, and then triumphantly adds that these are not ends in themselves. They are but illustrations of the fact that love works no ill against the neighbor; hence love is that which God really wants (Rom. 13:9-10). The effort to keep a set of rules governing one's conduct toward one's neighbor is a misunderstanding of the Christian faith. Legalism will not do. Rules without love are an offense to God, even if rigidly kept. Where love exists, it goes beyond all rules. It uses rules only as rough guidelines to the workings of love.

It is for this reason that we see in our Lord a habit of putting people above principles. When the sabbath became a block to neighbor-love, he set aside the contemporary rules for its observance, saying, "The sabbath was made for man, and not man for the sabbath." When men complained that his disciples picked corn on the sabbath, he reminded them of how David and his men, when hungered, had taken the showbread out of the house of God and had eaten it, which was unlawful to do. Yet our Lord told of the infraction with approval (Mark 2:24-27). Rules, principles, and institutions are but means to a larger end—love of people. If they fail to serve these larger ends and become ends in themselves, they must be set aside.

The love wherewith we are to love our neighbor is _agapē_-love. We have already seen that this love is not an ideal, but rather an ultimate reality, for God is this kind of love. It is this kind of love, therefore, which is shed abroad in our hearts through the Holy Spirit. _Agapē_-love does not negate the more earthy, craving kind of love with which we all are familiar, but it purifies it and releases it for its true function. Where craving love cannot go, as in love for enemies, _agapē_-love is always there. It is there, not as a feeling, but as an attitude. Christian love is not something to be felt, but something to be done in outgoing self-giving.

We saw something of the meaning of _agapē_-love when we spoke in the first chapter of God's love in Christ. In order that we may see more of what God intends for the redeemed man, let me here spell it out in detail as it relates to our conduct as Christians. _Agapē_-love is concerned. This, of course, is obvious. But if it is the love which we see in Christ, and if we are bidden to "walk in love, as Christ also hath loved us" (Eph. 5:2), we must quickly add that it is _infinitely_ and hence _imaginatively_ concerned. It goes _look-_

ing for opportunities to help. It sticks its neck out. It never merely plays it safe.

This infinite, imaginative love is tirelessly persistent. It never grows weary and gives up. It is like the fire which Moses saw burning so fiercely in the bush, yet not consuming the bush, because it did not feed upon the bush but upon itself (Ex. 3:1-6). *Agapē*-love does not feed upon the response of the one loved, drooping when an adequate response is withheld. Its energy is within its own nature, and hence it is tireless.

Agapē-love is unconditional. It does not say, "I'll love if. . . ." There are no "ifs," "ands," or "buts" about it. And because it is unconditional, it is all inclusive. It gives itself unreservedly, heedlessly, uncalculatingly to everyone, irrespective of who he is, or how unlovely, or how hostile. This all-embracing character of *agapē*-love is of the highest significance for the spread of love in human relations, for where love exists only within a certain group, it actually creates hostility and enmity on the part of those excluded. If it is only Americans that I love, non-Americans will resent my clannishness, particularly since such love will prompt me to push the advantage of my countrymen at the expense of the rest of the world. If it is only white people that I love, then colored people will resent my efforts to advance the white race at their expense. Love that is not unconditional and all-embracing is in itself a source of bitterness and enmity in society.

Agapē-love is nonsentimental. It does not (as so often happens in our semisecular churches) shove the difficult questions under the rug so that a façade of good fellowship can flourish in an atmosphere where no issues are faced, no prickly problems are grappled with, and no evils are attacked, but all is sweetness and light. Such a sentimental approach to people and problems does not promote Christian fellowship; it negates it by substituting for it mere genial familiarity. *Agapē*-love can wound as well as heal. It can hurt as a step toward helping. It includes as an essential part of it a concern for justice, while going beyond justice in intent and act.

Agapē-love is reconciling. Because it faces outward, affirming the rights of others ahead of its own, it takes the initiative in restoring broken relationships even when the fault is not its own.

This, then, is love. To love thus is to live the Christian life in relation to our fellowmen. How far this is from the I-go-to-church, pay-my-debts, live-a-good-life pitch with which we are all too painfully familiar! Who is sufficient for these things? It comes with something of a shock to be told by some that we all are!

While writing this chapter I have come across a newspaper article telling of the disagreements between two groups of Unitarians. One group wants to say that it preaches love of God and love of neighbor as the religion which Jesus taught, whereas the other group is satisfied to preach the same thing without special reference to Jesus. Both groups are in agreement that love of God and neighbor is a genuine possibility for not-so-sinful man. Thus they miss the point of biblical Christianity. "Love God and love your fellow man" is indeed the will of God for man and the summary of the Old Testament. But the fact that it comes to us in the form of a command, "Thou shalt love," shows that it is foreign to us. It is our duty, not a fact of our life. Love demanded as a duty and offered an an obligation sounds like a queer kind of love indeed. Hence, the New Testament brings between the love commandment and the person to whom it is addressed a gospel. If "love God and love your neighbor" summarizes the Old Testament, "Jesus died to make it so" summarizes the New. If the necessity for this last is not by now fully clear, it should become so when we bring the love commandment into relation with the first two aspects of redemption with which we dealt—redemption as forgiveness and redemption as wholeness.

In brief, the situation is this: Until I am made a whole person in the wholeness of Christ, I cannot see what love demands nor set about doing it. My own needs and perversions will distort my apprehension of the needs of others. Self-deception will rationalize away the urgency to act. Like the "certain lawyer" who, willing to justify himself, asked "Who is my neighbor?" we shall seek some means of dodging love's demands (Luke 10:29).

All too frequently we are but ministering to our own unconscious needs when we are talking about service in the name of Christian love. Who has not seen the belligerent "soul winner" who has a compulsive need to rearrange the lives of others? Who is not familiar with the "prophetic" preacher who ventilates his unconscious hostilities by attacking his congregation in the name of Jesus and his truth? Who is unfamiliar with the Christian worker whose great zeal in the work of the Lord masks an unconscious longing for the limelight or an equally unconscious need to expiate repressed guilt-feelings We are seemingly engaged in meeting the needs of others while actually meeting our own. Indeed, a recent sociological investigation of married love suggests that it is a far less "self-giving" than it appears to be. The author's thesis is that love between the sexes is basically self-serving. Each of us tends to fall in love with the type of person who complements his own personality and permits him to relieve his own frustrations by living vicariously in the life of the beloved with whom he identifies.[11]

The solution for the blindness of sin which makes us unable to see our neighbor in his need and unwilling to meet fully the needs we do see, is the healing love of Christ who himself faced life and the needs of his fellowmen without projecting upon the situation the distorting effects of pride, anxiety, and self-concern. Redemption-unto-love needs as its companion redemption-as-wholeness. We need to be made whole in the wholeness of Christ, that by his grace we may see clearly, be motivated adequately, and be enabled fully to exercise neighbor-love, in humility, patience, and hope. We need to let him take us off our own hands so that we can be released to serve others. Yet, even the love with which we thereafter love is none other than the Love which so loved the world. We love with the Love wherewith we *were* loved. Not what we do, but what he is able to do *through* us, is of enduring quality. In the last analysis, there is only one Worker in all the world. Our job is to let God work—through us and therefore in us.

But how can we face the bitter truth about ourselves without flinching and without despair? How can we bear the knowledge of our hypocrisy, self-deception, faithlessness, pride, lust, anxiety, status- and approval-drives, and all the rest? How, except as we stand in the presence of a Love which understands and forgives? It is only because the One with whom we have to deal is forgiving and merciful that we can look, take note with clear and single eye, acknowledge, and confess. "There is forgiveness with thee," cries the Psalmist. Because we have been and continue to be forgiven, we even find the strength to forgive and continue to forgive ourselves—a very difficult job as every counselor

[11] Robert F. Winch, *Mate Selection,* Harpers, 1959. The author's investigation covered 25 couples.

knows. Thus, redemption-as-forgiveness (especially as we remember that forgiveness includes restoration to God's fellowship) is a necessary component of redemption-as-wholeness and redemption-unto-love. These three are not three different operations but one mighty act of saving grace.

Now, implied in what we have been saying in the last few paragraphs is something that may have escaped the reader, namely that there is a Christian affirmation of self as well as a sinful love of self. Some theologians call this a legitimate and Christian self-love as opposed to a sinful self-love.

There would seem to be biblical authority for this, since our Lord speaks of loving thy neighbor "as thyself." But it is not wholly clear what Christ is saying here. Does this mean that you *should* love yourself, or is Luther right when he says this *forbids* loving yourself, because all of the energy once used in self-love is now to be directed toward the neighbor? Both sides have been argued. But even if Luther is wrong and his opponents right, it sounds highly misleading to use the same term, "self-love," to stand for sin on the one hand and Christianity on the other. The more modern term "self-acceptance" has also proved subject to misunderstanding. I, therefore, prefer to talk about Christian self-affirmation, which may be no better than the alternative phrases.

Whatever the term, something quite important is at issue: Is the Christian ideal selflessness or self-giving?

The advocates of selflessness have much toward which they can point in the way of verses like "deny self" and "I am crucified with Christ." Yet we must not let them have the last word, lest we give to the world the appearance of hating the personality and willing its death that Christ might be all. Christ must be all, all right. But he *is* all when a redeemed self, in glad thanksgiving, reports for duty. The self that must be crucified is the self as it is oriented and structured in opposition to God. That self must go, that a new self may be born, a self that loves God and seeks his will. Then, when the redeemed self gives itself in sacrifice for the cause of Christ, it is not because it despises itself or loathes itself. Rather it gives itself in devotion to the neighbor in full recognition of its own worth (if I may use the word) as a died-for, forgiven, renewed-in-God's-image product of the Divine Carpenter's skill. A man must learn to respect himself and even value himself not for his own sake (that would be sin indeed), but for the sake of Christ, whose love he must body forth, and of the neighbor on whose behalf he mediates Christ's love. Self-giving in love is of little value if the person making the gesture has no self worth giving!

The pattern for all this is none other than our Lord himself who, "knowing that the Father had given all things into his hands, and that he was come from God, and went to God . . . took a towel . . . and began to wash the disciples' feet" (John 13:3-5). He stooped, not because he was ignorant of who he was, but because he was fully aware. He died, not because he hated life and self, but in recognition of the worth of both. And to be redeemed by his grace is to acknowledge in glad surprise that by his mercies I have become worthful to God and therefore to myself. I must, then, learn to forgive myself when God has forgiven me, learn to live within my limitations except when God gives me grace to stretch them, be selective, under his guidance, of the tasks that I attempt, and eschew the temptation to play God to a sinking world. As though I could hold it in place by a frenzied juggling act in which I seek to keep aloft an ever-increasing number of accepted responsibilities!

I mention the problem of the overactive Christian worker because excessive activity is one way of expressing an unchristian self-hate. Frequently an overworked, overburdened Christian semiconsciously thinks (and overtly acts as though) his service to Chirst is more important than he. He therefore seeks to justify his existence by what he does in Christ's service—and ends up with a nervous breakdown. The glad good news of the gospel tells us that Christ loves us for ourselves, not for what he can get out of us. We work for him as friends (John 15:15), not as slaves, except as we become the willing slaves of love. All this is Christian self-affirmation, a prelude to Christian self-giving as opposed to neurotic self-giving or neurotic selflessness.

The link between self-affirmation and self-giving is love. It is the mystery of love that we are never so much ourselves as when we are giving ourselves away in concern for others. We never possess ourselves so completely as when we yield ourselves in love. Love breaks down separateness at precisely the same time that it heightens individuality. The more you give of yourself in love (not in self-loathing, nor in foot-dragging duty), the more you *are*—are in genuine, personal reality, richness, and awareness.

Such life-in-love, for which we are released in the gospel is life in the present tense. Emil Brunner has a choice little book called *Faith, Hope, and Love* in which he remarks on how human beings are capable of living in the past and the future as well as in the present. While their bodies are living in the Here and Now, their minds may be living in the Then and There. We may be spending our energies in either dreaming about (or regretting) the past or in dreaming about (or fearing) the future. Either way, the present moment, the only actual moment we ever have at our disposal, slips away from us. We are all familiar with the type of hard-driving man who never permits himself any fun or relaxation because he is making money so that he can do all the things he wants to do when he retires. Then retirement comes, and he finds that he has lost the ability to enjoy it. He has spent his life in chasing the future, and when the future comes he cannot take advantage of it because the only thing he knows is work.

This is one form of living in the wrong time-dimension. There are many other forms.

Now, what the gospel offers us is life. Life can only be lived now, in the only moment we ever actually possess. So Christ comes to us and says: "I'll worry about your past; you forget it. I took care of it at Calvary." Then he adds: "I'll take care of your future too; it's as bright as God's purposes." So, released from overanxiety in both directions, we are free to live moment by moment in the fullness of a life which hears God's call and answers it in love for the neighbor as each succeeding day gives opportunity. To love is to live *now*—present tense.

Redemption as Past Event

There is an old, old problem which many of us puzzled over in our high school physics. The problem is this: If a tree falls in the forest and there is no one there to hear it fall, is there any sound? It is clear that the question can be argued either way—depending on your point of view. Obviously, something happens; disturbance waves are set up in the air and they operate whether or not anybody is around. But if you define sound as the effect that such waves have on the receiving ear of a human being, then the formula will read, "No man, no sound."

The same problem arises in the Christian faith. Is there revelation whether or not anybody responds to the revelation? The answer is the same as above. If by revelation you mean that God has done something to catch men's attention and to disclose himself to them whether anybody heeds or not, then the answer is, Yes. But since God does not waste his time making revelations that fall flat on their face, it is easier to say that revelation is not complete until it finds the heart and soul of the believer. Yet we use the word "revelation" in both ways. We sometimes speak as though Jesus Christ was the revelation of God just by being what he was and doing what he did. But when we give further thought to it, we know that unless the God who stepped into our human story in Jesus Christ takes one step more and walks into our hearts, revelation has not effectively taken place. This "walking into our hearts," of course, is the work of the Holy Spirit. The Christ of history and the Christ of dogma must become the Internal Christ. What happened "back there" must end "in here."

Now we can play this same game of "back there" and "in here" with the word "redemption." Has the world been redeemed? Yes—and then again, No. The "No" is easily recognized. Multitudes who walk the earth are without God and without hope in the world. The world with its institutions and peoples staggers from one crisis to another, unable to resolve its tensions and heal its divisions. Crime, sin, shame, degradation, poverty—these are daily facts of our world. Obviously, in one sense, the world is far from being redeemed.

Yet in another sense it has been redeemed. Something not only of world-shaking, but of cosmos-shaking, significance took place "back there." The world's sin was atoned for. The enemies of man were put to rout. The power of evil was broken. The revolt of Satan was put down. After Calvary and Easter, things would never be the same again in God's great universe. Since that time, there's been a Man in the heavenlies.

In this chapter I have been interweaving the objective facts and the subjective effects in the human heart, the "back there" aspect and the "in here" aspect. But I would like for the stress of the chapter to fall on the "back there" element. It is the Christ who was, that captures our attention here. It is redemption as a past event upon which I wish to focus. It is what God did objectively—quite aside from man's response—which I want to underscore: I can summarize it quickly and clearly, I trust, in the framework of the threefold nature of sin within which we have been working: guilt, bondage, lovelessness.

Take guilt. Man could not solve the problem of his guilt. Shall he repent and live a good life ever after? But what is a "good life" and how shall he attain it? If there is an answer to this question, what of his past and its accumulated guilt? How does man wipe the slate clean of that? The fact is, man does not know the bankruptcy of his situation, the size of the debt he owes to God, or the price of reconciliation. The initiative must be God's. The sky-high barrier that sin had erected between God and man could not be torn down by man's small hand. Only God's hand was strong enough. It is not for man to speak the word of reconciling forgiveness; only the One sinned against could do that. The bridging of the gap between Holy God and sinful man for the purpose of effecting reconciliation was a God-sized job. And God did it! That's the gospel. Forgiveness is now a proffered fact—not an inference or a deduction.

Or take bondage. Here the New Testament makes clear that the problem is deeper than the mere fact of man's eccentricity and distortion. Sin is not merely an unfortunate mistake into which we fall at times. It is a mighty power which holds the whole race in its grip. Sin has become destiny and stands over against us as an objective force. We not only sin, but also are the slaves of sin. We all are bound together inexorably in the solidarity of sin. Likewise, death is an objective power. It is not merely that death is an event which closes our earthly life. It is an alien force which dominates us even while we live. For Paul, the very existence which we live is an existence which is captive unto Death. With Sin and Death is coupled the power of the Law, which makes demands upon us without lifting a finger to help. Nor is this all. Behind Sin, Death, and the bondage of Law stands a whole kingdom of Evil, the kingdom of Satan and of the "principalities and powers" of which Paul so frequently speaks. Thus, a whole evil dynasty was challenged at the Cross. All Hell moved up to block the redemptive move that Heaven was making.

The ensuing collision shook the foundations and when the smoke had cleared a Divine Victim was stretched helpless on a cross. The future of humanity hung in the balance. But the end was not yet. Sin, Law, Death, and the Devil had indeed done their worst. But their worst was not enough. Sin had failed to corrupt him, so Death could not hold him; and when he arose from the grave, he broke the tyranny of both. He was undisputed victor "o'er the dark domain." Sin, Death, and the Devil—all were under his feet. He "disarmed the principalities and powers and made a public example of them" (Col. 2:15, RSV). The powers of evil had met their master; their day had run its course. In the death and resurrection of Jesus Christ, something objective happened, happened "back there," that meant defeat for the forces of evil in the world and constituted Jesus Christ as Lord. From then on, his was the final authority over all things in the world.

Finally, take lovelessness. The apostle John says that "we love because he loved." Modern psychiatry has taught us part of the truth in that phrase. We now know that a person's inability to love can be cured only by his being on the receiving end of somebody else's love. Only as we are loved are we able to give love. Somebody else must bear the brunt of our unloveliness and unloveableness, if we are to be released to love others. So says psychology. And so says the cross. In the death of Jesus Christ something objective happened, happened "back there," that demonstrated the unspeakable love of God.

Andrew Jackson, later President of the United States, won early fame as the United States general in the Battle of New Orleans, the last great battle of the War of 1812. Actually the battle was fought, as we remember from our high school history, after the peace treaty was signed (though not yet ratified) in Europe, December 24, 1814. But news traveled so slowly in those days that Jackson in faraway Louisiana had not received the good news and so joined battle in early January of 1815. Had Jackson known, he might have confronted his foe with words like these: "I don't have to battle with you. You're already licked. The war is over. I take my stand on the victory of the United States government over all its enemies."

But Jackson did not know that the war was over. Similarly, the non-Christian does not know that the war of life is over and that every enemy of life has been put to rout in the redemption that was wrought "back there" in Jesus Christ. Or, to revert to the illustration of Denmark and the Nazis mentioned in the preceding chapter, he does not know that he has been delivered; and so he still hides out, living as best he can, cut off from home and hearth, in constant terror of life, in tormenting fear of death. It is the job of evangelism to tell him—and to tell him in such a way that he will really enter into the truth of the situation and abandon his former manner of life. "The Deliverer has come! Humanity is free!"

There is an arresting verse in Obadiah 1:17 that promises that "the house of Jacob shall possess their possessions." Possess their possessions. One would hope so! Yet every once in a while the papers speak of someone who has been left a sizable inheritance but cannot be found. He lives in ignorance of his good fortune and misses out on what is rightfully his. He is like those famous survivors of a lost ship at sea who, half-mad with thirst, begged the first ship that hove into sight for life-giving water only to be told with laughter that they were surrounded with it. They had unwittingly drifted into the fresh-water estuary of the Amazon river. Evangelism is the persistent effort to get people to take their blinders off and see where they are as the inheritors of the great possessions left them in the last will and testament of the Crucified One. Salvation is possessing one's possessions.[12]

---

[12] On the various theories of the atonement, see Appendix B.

THE CHRIST WHO IS

3

JESUS CHRIST IS LORD. This is the core dogma of the Christian faith. This is the truth which evangelism proclaims. This is the fact which confronts the world—Jesus Christ is Lord.

The tense is important. Now, right this moment, Jesus Christ, who was dead and was made alive again, *is* the Lord. He reigns now. He rules now. Opposition to him is futile. "For he must reign, till he hath put all enemies under his feet" (1 Cor. 15:25). By his death, resurrection, and exaltation he has atoned for the world's sin, broken the power of the enemy, and won for himself a kingdom. There is really only one Lord, one authority, one ruler—Jesus Christ. The heights are held by him who is the lover of our souls. Wonderful news this—the very evangel that we proclaim.

"We proclaim"? How did *we* get in on this? The answer is the irony of the centuries. When his opponents "did him in," they thought that they had got rid of him for good. They did not know that they had overreached themselves and had played right into his hands. They pushed him off the planet and right onto his Father's throne. The very first thing he did from that position of power was to form for himself a new body; and lo! he was back in business again—on earth. We got in on it by becoming members of his body, who filleth all in all. Thus, a major part of the biography of the Christ-who-is, the Christ who now reigns and rules as living Lord, is the story of his body, the church. So the church becomes part of the gospel which we proclaim.

A revolutionary idea, this, and one which surely cries for defense. The church is surely the *product* of the gospel; it is the place where the gospel has been heard gratefully, and hence where the gospel has taken hold. The church is the place where the Lordship of Christ is acknowledged, where his atoning mercies are operative, and where his forgiveness is sought. By his grace, we have entered into the salvation which he wrought at such cost. "Christ's offered life becomes the power of a perfect and glorified humanity, which from the unseen world can penetrate and transform human souls."[1] Paul says it differently, but he is affirming the same thing when he writes in Romans 5:10: "For if, when we were enemies, we were reconciled to God by the death of his Son, much more, being reconciled, we shall be saved by his life." Salvation means to be "in Christ," to be incorporated into his life, to be in union with him. We sometimes say that Christianity is not only a creed, but is also a life. This is true; but if we were to be specific, we would have to say that it is not *a* life, but *the* life, the life of God's New Order, the life of Jesus Christ himself, in which we participate. God's own life is in us; and he *is* Life. "When Christ, who is our life, shall appear . . . (Col. 3:4). Christ, the image of God, lives in the believer that the believer may be conformed to the image of the Son. Here the imperfect is gathered up into the Perfect that it may share that perfection. Here the perverted is lifted up into the Pattern that it may become like the Pattern.

Yet not the believer alone, but the believer along with his fellowbeliever in a shared salvation. For as Luther so clearly saw, if *I* am in Christ and *you* are in Christ, then we

[1] From *The Doctrines of the Creed,* by Oliver Quick (London: Nisbet & Co., Ltd., 1938), p. 235. Used by permission.

are also in each other. We shall never understand the New Testament until we stop thinking in terms of a series of individual "I" 's, each one being saved in isolation by Christ, and begin to get that "we" feeling. For while the Christian faith is _personal_, it is not _individual_. What's the difference? Simply this. While we each must make a personal decision of our own, we are saved in the togetherness of the whole people of God, the fellowship of believers.

Human life is corporate; it always has been, and always will be. G. Ernest Wright is surely correct when he says: "The biblical story must not be interpreted as the progressive emancipation of the individual, but instead as God's action in history to create a community in which the responsible individual finds his true being."[2] It is as true of a Christian as of a railroad ticket—not good if detached. All this is what that famous Baptist, Charles Haddon Spurgeon, meant when he spoke these arresting words:

> I am in the truest sense a very sound churchman. I am, indeed, a high churchman; a most determined stickler for the church. I do not believe in salvation outside the pale of the church. I believe that the salvation of God is confined to the church, and to the church alone. You say, "What church?" God forbid that I should mean either the Baptist, the Independent, the Episcopalian, the Presbyterian, or any other church; I mean the church of Christ, the company of God's chosen, the fellowship of the blood-bought, be they where they may, for them is provided the feast of fat things. There is but one church in heaven and earth, composed of those called by the Holy Ghost, and made anew by his quickening power.[3]

When the greatest event in the history of the world was over, when the redemptive deed of God in Jesus Christ was

[2] From _The Biblical Doctrine of Man in Society_, by G. Ernest Wright (London: Student Christian Movement Press, Ltd., 1954), p. 97. Used by permission.

[3] From _The Theology of Evangelism_, by Henry Cook (London: The Carey Kingsgate Press, Ltd., 1951), p. 112. Used by permission.

done, nothing was left as its consequence in history except a community—the church, the fellowship of faith, hope, and love. This community was made up of those who, having heard the gospel, believed unto the salvation of their souls. These found the Way.

So, from one standpoint, it is clear that the church is the community of the redeemed. These, having heard and responded to the gospel, are the product of it. As such, the church is one side of the gospel, the side which stands over against the world to judge and to save it. But this is not the whole story. The church is an ambiguous community. It is earthy—all too earthy. But it is also heavenly, gloriously heavenly. It has one foot firmly planted in history, but it also has one foot in heaven. It is part of the problem, but it is at the same time part of the solution. How can this be?

Let us put it this way. You can say, "We are in Christ," with its overtones of security, or you can say, "Christ is in us," with its overtones of dynamic activity. When you put it the latter way, you are emphasizing the present Lordship of Christ—in and over his body, which is the church. Through the church, the risen Lord continues his work of taking away the sins of the world. The redeemed community is also the redeeming community. "As my Father hath sent me, even so send I you" (John 20:21). The church, also, is the act of God in Jesus Christ. It is the incarnation of the Third Member of the Trinity, even as Jesus Christ is the incarnation of the Second Member of the Trinity. The church, which is his body, is the creation and incarnation of the Holy Spirit. Dr. Nels Ferré is surely right when he says, "The historic continuity through which God works is the Christian communion as the extension of the Incarnation, of the Atonement, and of the Resurrection."[4] These are exciting words. They are also dangerous words.

These are exciting words because they express the New Testament picture of the extraordinary closeness existing between Christ and his church.[5] This closeness is expressed in three great metaphors: the bride, the building, and the body. The church is the bride to which Christ gives himself. It is the building of which he is the cornerstone. It is the body of which he is the head. Under these metaphors, some startling statements emerge, especially under the last. For instance, hear Paul in 1 Corinthians 12:12: "For as the body is one, and hath many members, and all the members of that one body, being many, are one body: so also is Christ." Now, every expectation of the reader leads him to read at the end, "so also is the church." But what Paul actually says is, "so also is Christ." As a head severed from a body leaves both incomplete, so does Christ the Head, if severed from his body, the church. Each is incomplete without the other. To put it differently, it takes Christ (the Head) and the church (his body) to make a whole Christ. Wonderful thought!

But these are also dangerous words, as Karl Barth and others have pointed out. We are in danger of forgetting that this is a metaphor, and that since it is such, we must not draw from it the conclusion which the Roman Catholic Church has drawn: namely, the institution to which I belong

[4] From *Protestantism: A Symposium*, Wm. K. Anderson, ed. (Nashville: The Methodist Church, Copyright, 1945), p. 283. Used by permission. See also *Return to Christianity*, by Nels Ferré (New York: Harper and Brothers, Copyright, 1943), pages 41-43.

[5] I surely do not need to point out that I am not talking about an organization or an institution, but about the fellowship of the redeemed. On the other hand, we must not make the fellowship so spiritual and invisible that we overlook the fact that unless the fellowship is organized for work and worship, it is unable to function. The institution and the fellowship are not the same, but they are related.

is Christ on earth—wielding his power, hurling his thunder-bolts, exercising his Lordship for the aggrandizement and greater glory of the institution. We must always remember the gap that exists between us, as the community of faith, hope, and love, and Jesus Christ. We are not the Word made flesh, but we can body forth his words. We are not the atoning Savior of the world, but we can fill up that which is lacking in the sufferings of Christ (Col. 1:24). We have not risen from the dead, but we can manifest his resurrection life.

Exciting . . . and dangerous. Like him . . . and unlike him. Both these truths must be kept in balance. For it is as possible to stress the *unlike* and forget the *like* as it is to stress the *like* and ignore the *unlike.* We are not identical with Christ, yet in a very real way we are his extension, for he is our life and Lord. Because we have been formed and fashioned to be his extension in history, we are part of the gospel. Christ offers himself-in-the-church for the needs of the world. We exist as the act of God and the gift of God to our age. We too are what God has done for man in Jesus Christ. To proclaim the gospel is to proclaim the good news that there is a people of God that stands in the world *for* the world, in Jesus' name. For Christ is Lord in the church and over the church for the sake of the world. To be a Christian is to acknowledge this Lordship. No form of evangelism that does not bring men to this commitment is New Testament evangelism.

"All authority in heaven and on earth has been given to me. Go therefore . . ." (Matt. 28:18f, RSV). These words, although addressed to the church, are of decisive importance to the world. They assert that Jesus Christ is Lord over everything, over the world as well as over the church. But the church hears the claim and obeys; the world does not.

What does it mean to say that Jesus Christ is Lord of

history, Lord over the world as well as over the church? In detail, I do not know. Even where somewhat general terms would be satisfactory, I am rarely satisfied with what the theologians try to spell out. We shall be on safer grounds if we do not speculate too radically here. What *is* clear is that somehow, in ways beyond our seeing, the purposes of God are going forward to their destined end. Furthermore, this is being accomplished against great opposition. Cullmann reminds us that the kingship of Christ over the world is a time of conflict. This is made clear in 1 Corinthians 15:23-28, RSV). Christ is to wield the power of God until "every rule and every authority and power" that opposes has been brought to destruction (vs. 24), then he will step down and the fullness of the rule of God over his redeemed creation will begin (vss. 25 and 28). Meanwhile, God has put everything in subjection under the feet of Christ (vs. 27) who is Lord of all, including those who keep muttering, "We will not have this man to reign over us." The world cannot escape involvement with the gospel. The One of whom the gospel speaks is its Lord.

How Christ works in history outside the agency of the church is beyond our knowing, and, besides, is none of our business! He can make the wrath of men to serve him. But his *main* instrument is the church, his body, which he has every right to depend on, for he fashioned it for exactly this purpose. Here our orders are clear. We exist for the *world.* It is the world which God so loved—and loves. The world is our field of operation.[6] The Lord of life and history, the crucified, risen, and exalted One is the Evangelist who uses us as his instruments, by means of the Holy Spirit, to bring

[6] Here I am using the term "world," not as I used it in the last chapter when speaking of it in its sinister sense ("Love not the world . . . ," "Be not conformed to this world," etc.), but as a synonym for people and their lives and activities. There is more than one Greek word used in the New Testament for what is translated as "world."

the world to himself. Our job is to make him known, or, better stated, to set up the conditions which make it possible for him to make himself known. We are "for the praise of his glory." We are on "the inside," and know that he plans to unite all things in himself (Eph. 1:9ff). We are not only aware of the plot as spectators, but also are part of it as actors.

The Church as a Mothering Community

A quick resumé. The gospel is the whole Christ-story and includes the Christ of the past, the Christ of the present, and the Christ of the future. The story of the Christ of the present, the Lord of History, inevitably involves the church, which is his body on earth. He formed and indwells the church through his Spirit, the Holy Spirit. The church is the act of God in Jesus Christ. It is part of what God offers the world, as the gift of his love. The church is part of the gospel which it preaches, part of the good news of Jesus Christ. What this means we must now consider in detail.

First of all, it is great good news that there exists on earth a mothering community where the deep need of men for fellowship, understanding, security, and love—across all artificial barriers—can be met. (If one wishes, he can call it instead a brothering community. But the love of a mother is usually deeper than that of a brother, and there is a strong tradition running all the way back to the early church fathers for calling the church "our mother.")

Children need these things; all children do. That is why the family is so important for society. We now know that where a child is robbed of love and understanding, he may be a crippled personality for life. It has been said that "love is like sunshine; it causes the organism to unfold." Lack of love is the cause of all manner of personality quirks and neuroses. Love is as important for the development of the personality as food for the body. Recent tests at the University of Wisconsin suggest that, if experiments with baby monkeys are any indication, the love of a tiny baby for the mother to whom it clings is based more on the comfort of contact than on the fact that the mother gives him food.

How vital for both psychic and bodily processes love is, is shown by the study that René Spitz, an American psychoanalyst, made in a South American foundling home where ninety-seven babies, ranging in age from three months to three years, lived. They were adequately fed and medically attended, but the shortage of nurses robbed them of the little loving attentions that most babies get. Most of the day they were left to themselves. Within three months, grave symptoms of abnormality began to emerge. Loss of appetite, loss of sleep, and loss of interest in life ensued. By the end of five months the deterioration had accelerated. Physically, most of them had shrunk beyond recognition. Emotionally starved, they whimpered and trembled, their faces twisted in grotesque ways. Twenty-seven of these children died in their first year and seven more in their second. Of those who lived, twenty-one were so affected that they were hopeless neurotics or worse. One harrowing film was taken of a doctor trying to comfort a fifteen-months-old youngster. The baby screams in panic, holding on to him with one hand for support, while with the other she beats him in terror. Her face is the face of an idiot, driven insane by loneliness and fear.

Truly, love is the very stuff of life. Growing toward maturity should mean a lessening need (though not a lessening desire) to receive love from all quarters and an increased ability to give love. But love remains at the heart of life. The mature ability to give and receive love lies at the basis of a successful marriage. Men have even dreamed of organizing society on the basis of genuine love-toward-neighbor.

This dream is one aspect of the appeal of Marxism. Its famous phrase, "From each according to his ability; to each according to his need," is a slogan for organizing the whole of social and economic life on a family basis. The utopian character of this appeal is obvious. But the fact that it speaks to a deep and wistful desire in human nature is significant. Men hunger for fellowship, for an end to strife, war, hatred, and bitterness. Men long for a community of brothers.

So does God! He made man in, through, and for love. If sin has ruined things it is not going to be permitted to exist forever. God is engaged in a long-range plan to build the community of brothers, the kingdom of God triumphant. Meanwhile, he has inserted into history a kind of interim kingdom of God, a fellowship of love and brotherhood. This brotherhood, this family of God, is both a down payment on his pledge to finally unite all things in Christ (Eph. 1:10) and a show-window demonstration of what he intends in Christ when all things find their perfection in him.

The church, the divine fellowship of believers, is that family of God. The inner meaning of the Christian faith is fellowship. This is clear from 1 John 1:3. There John states that the purpose of their declaration of the gospel is that "ye also may have fellowship with us"; and then he adds that "our fellowship is with the Father, and with his Son Jesus Christ." Deity itself, in Christianity, is a societal term—Father, Son, and Holy Spirit. To become a Christian is to be caught up into fellowship with the triune God and at the same time into fellowship with other believers who constitute the family of God—a family which transcends the boundaries of the biological family and binds men of diverse background, education, nation, and race into a unity by the melting power of the love of Christ. "And all that believed," we read in Acts 2:44, "were together." Of course they were! They shared a common experience, a common life, a common hope, a common task, a common loyalty, a common destiny. Something new had appeared in history—the community of *agapē*-love.

It is good news, a part of the great good news of the gospel, that there exists in the world this family of God. As the mothering community, it gathers all new-born babies in Christ into an accepting fellowship which provides the nourishment, understanding, and guidance which makes growth possible. The church as the providing family of God for new Christians is the New Environment for all those whose face and faith are set toward God. They that have left house and brethren, wife, sisters, and parents for Christ and the gospel's sake have received house and brethren, wife, sisters, and parents as Jesus promised (Mark 10:29-30).

When we have grown to Christian maturity, we still are in the family, even though our relation to it then is as adults-in-Christ rather than as babes-in-Christ. A friend of mine, sick in bed, was called on by an extraordinarily busy fellow-Christian to see how he was getting along. The sick man protested that his visitor should not have taken the time and trouble to come. But the visitor put the matter in perspective by saying: "Don't forget. I'm responsible for you." This is exactly the meaning of Christian community. The church, the family of God, is the place where children of God—erring, sinning, yet forgiven and striving—learn to take mutual responsibility for one another.

In the church, people in various stages of Christian growth, all of whom are in pilgrimage and none of whom have arrived, learn to love each other "in spite of" as well as "because of." There, in our common unworthiness, we are nonetheless wanted and accepted. God, who is so concerned for right relations, makes us members of the Fellowship of

Right Relations, where together we can explore the meaning of, the difficulty of, and also the joys of proper relatedness to our fellows in the bonds of Christ and in his common forgiveness. There growth in grace means growth in a fuller and heavier acceptance of responsibility-in-love toward the brethren. Maturity reveals itself in the increasing ability to give of ourselves and the decreasing need always to be on the receiving end of somebody else's love. We saw in Chapter 2 that a human being is constituted by his relationships. God takes these relationships so seriously that under normal conditions the love of Christ is mediated to the Christian largely through the love of the brethren, i.e., through the fellowship of the redeemed.

The importance of the family idea as applied to the church is shown in an interesting passage on ethics in Ephesians 4:25 and following. Paul has been speaking of the putting on of the new man, which is "created in righteousness [right relations with men] and true holiness [right relations with God]" (vs. 24). He then adds: "Wherefore putting away lying, speak every man truth with his neighbour: *for we are members one of another*" (vs. 25). The italicizing is mine, not Paul's. Its purpose is to pinpoint the reason Paul gives for not lying. The reason is *not* that such lying violates our highest ideals, but rather that it breaks the fellowship. It destroys the unity of the family. I cannot be a true brother when I cannot be trusted to be open and aboveboard. This is but one example of several that point up the same truth. In verse 28, the appeal to stop stealing is implicitly grounded in the same argument, but it takes the more positive form of stressing that if you work, you will have money to give to your brothers who are in need; i.e., you will be able to advance the fellowship. When, next, Paul speaks of avoiding corrupt communication, he puts the prohibition in the same context. Speech is for the purpose of helping the brethren to grow in Christ; "corrupt communication" tears down the fellowship (vs. 29). In these passages, ethics is based, not on some impersonal moral law, but on the living interpersonal intimacies of the Fellowship of Right Relations. The ethic is a fellowship ethic. We are members one of another.

Let me conclude this section by giving a picture of the seriousness with which the early church took its life of brotherhood. It is taken from the writing of an early skeptic, Lucian of Samosata, as related by Friedrich Engels. The story concerns a young man called Peregrinus, or alternatively, Proteus. He became identified with the Christian church (Lucian considered him a fraud) and was elevated to a position of leadership in it.

> On that ground [i.e., because he was a Christian] Proteus was at length arrested by the authorities and thrown into prison. . . . As he thus lay in chains, the Christians, who saw in his capture a great misfortune, made all possible attempts to free him. But they did not succeed. Then they administered to him in all possible ways with the greatest solicitude. As early as daybreak one could see the aged mothers, widows, and young orphans crowding at the door of the prison; the most prominent among the Christians even bribed the warders and spent whole nights with him; they took their meals with him and read their holy books in his presence; briefly, the beloved Peregrinus [he still went by that name] was no less to them than a new Socrates. Envoys of Christian communities came to him even from towns in Asia Minor to lend him a helping hand, to console him, and to testify in his favor in court. *It is unbelievable how quick these people are to act whenever it is a question of their community; they immediately spare neither exertion nor expense.* And thus from all sides money then poured in to Peregrinus, so that his imprisonment became for him a source of great income. For the poor people persuaded themselves that they were immortal in body and in soul, and that they would live for all eternity; that was why they scorned death and many of them even voluntarily sacrificed their lives. Then their most prominent lawgiver convinced them that they would all be brothers one to another once they were converted, i.e., renounced the Greek

gods, professed faith in the crucified sophist, and lived according to his prescriptions. That is why they despise all material goods without distinction and own them in common—doctrines which they have accepted in good faith, without demonstration or proof. And when a skillful imposter who knows how to make clever use of circumstances comes to them he can manage to get rich in a short time and laugh up his sleeve over these simpletons. For the rest, Peregrinus was set free by him who was then prefect of Syria.

[Then, after a few more adventures] our worthy set forth a second time [from Parium] on his peregrinations, the Christians' good disposition standing him in lieu of money for his journey; they administered to his needs everywhere, and never let him suffer want. He was fed for a time in this way. But then when he violated the laws of the Christians, too—I think he was caught eating of some forbidden food—they excommunicated him from their community.[7]

THE CHURCH AS A MINISTERING COMMUNITY

Although the love of Christ finds its initial embodiment in the church, it inevitably spills over from the church to the world. Furthermore, if it is part of the great good news of the gospel that there exists a household of God in whose fellowship men may find love and acceptance, it is equally important news that there exists in the world a people who are the hand of God for the doing of his works of love. The church is not only a mothering community (this is its internal operation), but also it is a ministering community (this is its external operation). The church is not only a gathered community; it is also a scattered community. The church, like a harbor, is not only a fellowship into which people come, but also a fellowship from which people go out. Or better and more accurately, the church is not only a community called to Christ's side; it is also a community

[7] F. Engels, "On the History of Early Christianity," in *Basic Writings on Politics and Philosophy* (New York: Doubleday & Company, Inc., Copyright, 1959), ed. by Lewis Feuer, p. 171f. Used by permission. The italics are by the author.

sent from Christ's side in his name and in his behalf. "As my Father hath sent me, even so send I you." The church is apostolic in its very nature—"apostolic" being a word whose root meaning is "sent forth with orders." It is sent forth to do the will of its Lord, to carry on the ministry of the Suffering Servant.

We must be very clear on this point. Our exalted Lord was the humble Jesus. His ministry was the ministry of the Suffering Servant, not of the mighty conqueror. He was to "win through" by a cross, not by a sword or a popularity contest. It is the mission of his body, the church, to be the church of the Suffering Servant. It is either *this* kind of church or it is not a church of Jesus Christ at all. Some day we shall reign with him, but only after we have shared his cross and suffered for him in a ministry patterned after his own. The church does not function as a powerful political group, or as an institution that, throwing its weight around, demands special privileges and attention from the world because it represents Almighty God. It remains under the injunction of Christ, "Whosoever of you will be the chiefest, shall be servant of all" (Mark 10:44).

It is not surprising, then, to find in the New Testament the heavy emphasis on the ministry of good works. From a wealth of specific verses enjoining to good works, I choose a representative few. Take Ephesians 2:8-10: "By grace are ye saved through faith; and that not of yourselves: it is the gift of God: not of works, lest any man should boast. For we are his workmanship, created in Christ Jesus unto good works, which God hath before ordained that we should walk therein." The passage is clear: We are not saved *by* good works, but we are definitely saved *for* them. Or take that famous passage on the Scriptures: "All scripture is given by inspiration of God, and is profitable for doctrine, for reproof, for correction, for instruction in righteousness:

that the man of God may be perfect, throughly furnished unto all good works" (2 Tim. 3:16-17). Here again the meaning is clear. The end result of what Scripture can do for the man of God is to equip him for every good work. Or take Titus 2:13-14: "Looking for that blessed hope, and the glorious appearing of the great God and our Saviour Jesus Christ; who gave himself for us, that he might redeem us from all iniquity, and purify unto himself a peculiar people, zealous of good works." Once more, the end result of the sacrifice of Christ was a redeemed and purified people that would be—a ministering community!

Robert Luccock has his own effective way of saying it:

> In the Catskill Mountains back of Kingston, New York, is a road that winds along a hillside bordering an exquisitely lovely lake. Near a place where many stop to drink in the beauty of the scene with its cool breath of forest and sky is a sign: "Ashokan Reservoir—New York City Water Supply." Your mind makes the journey of 90 miles to the south and you realize that the real business of this lake is not to provide anyone's private aesthetic enjoyment. It is to quench the thirst and cleanse the stain of a whole city of men. Here is a reservoir flowing down from majestic mountains through a long aqueduct and out into millions of blighted homes and lives with refreshment, cleansing, and new life. So it is with God's love. To the sink holes of iniquity in our great cities, to the compounds of despair where humanity huddles in fear across Asia and Africa, to the places where men devise evil against their fellows in lands of totalitarian bondage, to the brokenhearted who cry in the long watches of the night—this is where the love of God drains.[8]

And it drains through *us!* Let us not forget it.

How does the church set about being the minister of God's loving concern? At this point I do not want to mention "speaking to a man about Christ" as an expression of loving concern. I want to leave the evangelizing word for treatment later in this chapter. Here I want to confine my-

[8] From *If God Be for Us*, by Robert Luccock (New York: Harper and Brothers, Copyright, 1954). Used by permission.

self to deeds and deeds alone. How does the church set
about its ministry of good works?

We can touch lightly on the first answer to this and then
pass on—not because the first answer deals with a matter of
small importance, but because there is no controversy about
the worth of that approach. Everyone agrees, so we can
merely refer to it and leave it there. I am talking about
the ministry of the cup of cold water given in Christ's name
—the individual acts of kindness done by Christians (or by
the church) for the sake of the troubled and unfortunate.
This is certainly part of our ministry of concern.

The ministry of the cup of cold water can usually be
done only as an over-and-above, that is to say, in our leisure
time. It inevitably partakes of the casual and occasional. But
there is a service to our neighbor which we can render day
after day, week after week, month after month, and year
after year. This is the service we render, not after the working day is over, but while it is going on. It is neighbor-love
in and through the actual job that we hold.

The church has always seen this for some occupations—
such as minister, nurse, doctor, and perhaps even housewife,
if we can place this in the same classification with the others.
Indeed, it is the desire to be of service to Christ and the
neighbor through their lifework that gives some young
people the urge to seek out the ministry or the mission field
or something similar. As second best, they will settle for
the secular professions of doctor, lawyer, etc. What I am now
suggesting is that this division between service professions
and non-service professions is most unfortunate. It would
mean, if valid, that some Christians can have a meaningful
lifework, but that other Christians are barred from it. The
Christian grocery clerk and the Christian pipefitter are out
of luck, that's all. They can only hope to do something
Christian in their spare time, not through their jobs.

I shall have more to say about this later. For the present, a quote from Luther will point up the truth that any job which is necessary and helpful to the functioning of society (there are some that are not helpful) is a means whereby the Christian can serve his neighbor in love. In it Luther suggests that the things that constitute our on-the-job tools serve as a kind of Bible at this point, to guide our thinking and living:

> To use a rough example: If you are a craftsman you will find the Bible placed in your workshop, in your hands, in your heart; it teaches and preaches how you ought to treat your neighbor. Only look at your tools, your needle . . . your articles of trade, your scales, your measures, and you will find this saying written on them. You will not be able to look anywhere where it does not strike your eyes. None of the things with which you deal daily are too trifling to tell you this incessantly, if you are but willing to hear it; and there is no lack of such preaching, for you have as many preachers as there are transactions, commodities, tools, and implements in your house and estate; and they shout this to your face, "My dear, use me toward your neighbor as you would want him to act toward you with that which is his."[9]

This form of Christian service is not very exciting and people, as a rule, are not thankful for it. But Luther has an answer to that too. God's love is a love which scatters its gifts upon a thankless world. At God's bidding, not only the sun and the rain, but the berries, trees, singing birds, and flowers give themselves to all who pass by, however unworthy. "For whom do I bear my delicious fruit or berry? For the worst rogues and rascals on earth!" This is the pattern for Christian love, which also must be willing to be misused, and to be a "lost love."[10]

There is a third way of doing good deeds. That is through

[9] Luther, *The Sermon on the Mount.* Quoted by Gustave Wingren (Carl Rasmussen, translator), in *Luther on Vocation* (Philadelphia: The Muhlenberg Press, Copyright, 1957), p. 72. Used by permission.

[10] *Ibid.* See Wingren, *op. cit.,* p. 170.

the ministry of social action. This is the most controversial form of the three, so it merits some further investigation. Let us begin with the story of the Good Samaritan (Luke 10:30-37). Parenthetically, if you listened to some people, you would get the impression that they feel very unhappy about having this story in the New Testament; it clearly bothers them terribly—no "gospel" in it (the Christian life, after the acceptance of the gospel, apparently being no concern of theirs). But that is another story. Let us look at the story we have before us—that of the Good Samaritan. A man fell among thieves, was ignored by some who passed by, but finally was picked up and ministered to by a neighborly fellow from Samaria (a very unpopular area with greatly disliked inhabitants). But that too is another story. As Jesus tells the tale, it is clearly a case of the first type of good works mentioned above—the ministry of individual acts of kindness to those in need.

But suppose the story had continued further. Suppose the Good Samaritan, later, had formed a committee—the Committee for Making the Jericho Road a Safe Highway. Suppose the committee had put on a big publicity campaign and had forced City Hall to string lights along the Jericho Road, to remove the shrubbery in which the thieves were accustomed to hide before pouncing, and to increase the number of policemen who patrolled the road. Why, oh why, would not this too be a form of neighbor-love? And if City Hall refused because it was in cahoots with the thieves, who regularly "paid off" the politicians, would it not be an act of kindness to all potential future victims for the committee to agitate for the removal of the grafters in the next election and the installation of an administration which would do these things? If the motive were the same—for love of Christ and the neighbor—would not this, too, be a form of Christian good deeds? True, this involves corporate action rather than individual action and therefore is a kind of love-at-a-distance (as someone has defined "justice"), being more indirect. But what of that? How many kinds of good works are *exempted* from the injunction to perform "all good works"?

The fact of the matter is that social problems play a large part in the biblical record. Most of them are in the Old Testament, but they are not found exclusively in the Old Testament. James once preached against the rich who exploited their workers by not giving them a fair wage (James 5:4)—a kind of preaching which, had he tried it in the typical Baptist church of today, would have caused a committee of the deacons to wait on him with the request that he please stick to the gospel and avoid discussing economics.

What a difference between the "biblical preachers" of today and the biblical preachers of the Bible! True, an Isaiah or a Jeremiah, while being no less biblical, would not preach in just the same way if they lived on this side of the gospel of Christ. But you would expect that the modern preacher of the Bible would have *something* in common with the great revealers of the will and truth of God whose prophetic utterances make up so important a part of the Old Testament. From Moses, with his regulations for social life and his social ethics, on through Amos, Isaiah, Jeremiah, and other of the prophets, you find a tremendous concern for social righteousness. For those who may never have read any of the ancient prophets, a few illustrative passages will prove illuminating. Here is one of scores of such passages from Isaiah:

> Is not this the fast that I [God] choose:
>> to loose the bonds of wickedness,
>> to undo the thongs of the yoke,

to let the oppressed go free,
  and to break every yoke? (Isa. 58:6, RSV);

or again:

For I the Lord love justice,
  I hate robbery and wrong . . . (Isa. 61:8, RSV).

And again:

He [a previous king] judged the cause of the poor and needy;
  then it was well.
Is not this to know me?
  says the Lord (Jer. 22:16, RSV. Italics mine).

To hear some people tell it, God has changed since he became a Christian. They talk as though God has outgrown all interest in justice and righteousness since Jesus came. They imply that indignation against injustice, oppression, poverty, and wrong was merely part of God's callow youth!

Our Lord did not so neatly separate the Old Testament from the New. He *reaffirmed* the witness of the prophets; then went on to make his own specialized contribution. The Old Testament was his Bible, the very Word of God to him. The God of the Old Testament prophets was precisely the God he came to make fully known. He *endorsed* the social character of the Old Testament teachings in order to add to it the personalized necessity of a new birth, and to provide the atonement which made it possible. Our Lord, in his own earthly mission, did not identify himself with the priestly vocation of the Old Testament but with the prophetic. When he stated his mission at the very beginning of his ministry in the famous synagogue episode recorded in Luke 4, he did so in the social terms of a quotation from Isaiah: "The Spirit of the Lord is upon me, because he hath anointed me to preach the gospel to the poor; he hath sent me to heal the brokenhearted, to preach deliverance to the captives, and recovering of sight to the blind, to set at liberty them that are bruised, to preach the acceptable year of the

Lord" (Luke 4:18-19). This announcement of his mission must not be completely spiritualized away. We have no right to do so when the record makes it clear that he did all of these things literally and physically, as well as spiritually. He *did* unbind the captives of disease, death, and demons. He *did* open the eyes of the physically blind. The assumption that all he was doing in the pronouncement at the synagogue was saying the same thing in four different ways—the spiritually poor, the spiritually brokenhearted, the spiritual captives, and the spiritually blind—is unlikely on the face of it.

But Jesus did more than take for granted the vast social concern interwoven through the pages of his own revered Bible—the Old Testament. He *fulfilled* it, as he did so many other things in the Old Testament revelation. It is of vital importance to our argument that we see this. You will remember that in the last chapter we noted that Paul showed that the moral law had been fulfilled in Christ, for love is the fulfilling of the law (Rom. 13:8-10; and Gal. 5:14). Thus, when you have said, "Love thy neighbor," you have said also, "Don't commit adultery," "Don't kill," "Don't steal," "Don't bear false witness," "Don't covet," and much more. Now, precisely the same thing is true of the moral law on the social level. When you have said, "Love thy neighbor," you have said "Be like Amos and Isaiah and Jeremiah, and in God's name oppose all unrighteousness, injustice, oppression, corruption in high places, exploitation of the poor, etc." Can I prove that this interpretation is correct? I can. Our Lord himself summarized the inner meaning of the Old Testament as love of God and love of neighbor, and added, "On these . . . hang all the law *and the prophets*" (Matt. 22:40).

We can now see why there is so little said in the New Testament about social problems. It would not have been very relevant anyway, since Palestine was occupied by a foreign power and the early Christians had no voice in the government or in the management of affairs. In this matter their position was very different from that of the Old Testament prophets. Also it was very different from that of the Christian today in modern America, who is part of a democracy and by no means is a member of a despised minority. The Christian church in America cannot dodge, though it gives every indication of trying to do so, its responsibility for the character of American society.

The Old Testament prophets grounded their social concern, not in something temporary or transitional, but in the very character of God. We Christians worship the same God; and we have, moreover, a clear mandate for social concern in the will of God that his redeemed people be a community of *agapē*-love, to the honor of his name and the good of the neighbor. And love finds a way, as a foolish little make-believe will make clear. Suppose a frightened little bride, having kissed her husband goodbye on his first day to work, begins to fuss and worry about how she should greet him when he returns that evening. Do you also kiss your husband when he returns from work, or is it enough to have sent him off with this gesture of affection? She thumbs through the *Bride's Book* which the pastor had given her at the wedding. Nothing there. She looks through every book she had bought on how to be a successful wife. Nothing there. She wracks her little brain to see if she can think of anything the pastor had said about it when they had gone to him for premarital counseling. She remembers nothing. So when her husband came home that night she refused to kiss him!

It is a ridiculous parable. But is it any more ridiculous than for the church, having been told that it is the purveyor of the stooping, reconciling, sacrificing love of God, to turn its back on all the works of love in the social area by saying, "Show me where it is spelled out in black and white in the New Testament or I won't bother"? It is difficult to see how a man can be loved with *agapē*-love without the lover being concerned when that man, because of the color of his skin, is denied his rights by white people and cannot get decent housing for his family (the race problem), or is poverty stricken because he is being exploited (the economic problem) or sees his little boy killed by a drunken driver (the liquor problem), or finds himself attacked on the street by a gang of juvenile delinquents (the crime problem). I repeat, it is difficult, yet it has been attempted.

Action against the great social evils of our age is not only enjoined by the love of God which is shed abroad in our hearts through the Holy Spirit, it can also be seen as a way of affirming the lordship of Christ. It is not that Jesus Christ *will* be Lord (though that too is true), but that he *is* Lord. Therefore the believing church insists that in every area he have the pre-eminence. Unbelieving men do not know God's will in Christ. The church does, and insists that the world give heed to it. Anything which is contrary to Christ and his lordship must be fought by the church. What he is against, we too must be against. What he is for, we too must affirm. We cannot be for Christ without being against sin, wherever it is found.

Since to some this whole defense of social action may be somewhat new, it might be wise if we looked at the reasons why heretofore some of the very best Christians in our churches have shied away from this area.

One reason is the complexity of the problems. It is clear that a hungry man should be fed. It is not so clear what the Christian conscience should recommend for adjusting our economy so that there will be fewer depressions and less unemployment. This takes an expert to know—and even they sometimes disagree. So meanwhile the well-meaning Christian stays out of areas where some technical competence seems to be required. One must be sympathetic here (as long as this attitude is genuine and not a mere rationalization of an urge to be left alone). The problem points up the need of Christian economists, sociologists, and political scientists to explore areas of social concern with a view to helping the Christian church see the issues and grapple with them. It must be added at once that there are other social areas that are not so complex but what a layman could quickly orient himself for effective action, if he would but take the time to do a little studying and investigating.

② A second reason for backing away from it all is the impersonality of it. The good Samaritan could see whom he was helping. The experience was personalized. But the Committee for Making the Jericho Road a Safe Highway appears to be dealing with a situation rather than with people. But is it not obvious that this is not really so? What the committee is doing is saving *many* people from becoming victims of thieves. Actually they are helping more people than the good Samaritan helped. But because (in this case) the work is preventive on the one hand and impersonal on the other ("everybody" has no name), the people who need to get emotionally stirred by some concrete case are left cold. What it is important to note here is, first, that Christian love is not an emotion. We should not have to depend on emotion for activation, but on loyalty to Christ the Lord. Second, a so-called "social problem" is just a problem of a lot of individuals written large. One has not abandoned a concern for individuals when he engages in social action. It is because of the individuals caught in the situation that the concern arises. The fact that you cannot call these individuals by name has nothing to do with it.

A third reason, closely allied to the one we have just

mentioned, is an excessive trust in individualism. There are some issues that cannot be settled by buttonholing people one by one and asking them to behave. Halford Luccock once said that if every one in town dug a well in his back yard, the result would not be a municipal water system. A municipal water system can only be established by *corporate* action. Corporate evils usually can be eliminated only by corporate action. If we had waited to get rid of slavery until every last slaveholder, non-Christian as well as Christian, was persuaded that it was morally right to set his slaves free, we would have been waiting yet. Social evils acquire a socially entrenched character which gives them a kind of independent life of their own. Like segregation, they become a way of life that traps the individuals in it and from which only a few hardy souls can escape.

I should add that there is a kind of grim irony about the way this excessive trust in individualism works. Its slogan usually is, "Changed individuals will change society." But ironically, when a changed individual sets out to change society, his worst enemies usually are the very ones who have been chanting so hypnotically, "Changed individuals will change society"! Individualists need to be reminded that the term, "kingdom of God," is a *corporate* term—though, of course, the kingdom is entered by personal decision.

A fourth reason is a historical one. The memory of the social gospel movement of another day, with its defective theology and its talk about "bringing in the kingdom," has caused many of the older generation in our churches to look with suspicion on all forms of social action. I shall have more to say about this shortly, when I come to speak of the church's witness, but for the present two comments will suffice. The first is this: We should not be against something merely because those we disapprove of are *for* it. In the

Communist Manifesto, Karl Marx spoke out for "free education for all children in public schools." His approval of free education is no reason for our disapproval. Secondly, I have said nothing in this chapter about "bringing in the kingdom," or substituting social action for the new birth, or about any of the other things for which the social gospel was attacked. I have merely sought to show that Christ's authority and Christian love demand action on the part of the church as a ministering community.

There is a fifth reason which I can touch on quickly, namely, that since unbelieving humanists can get all excited about race relations, international problems, etc., there cannot be anything very Christian about this area. Here again two things need to be said. One, the same objection could be raised—but, interestingly enough, is not raised—against doing the little individual kindnesses that all Christians acknowledge to be their duty. Unbelievers often do deeds of kindness too, even to the giving of a cup of cold water. The difference—and this is similarly true of social concern—is the motive. Neither the giving of a cup of water nor the attacking of a social evil is Christian in and of itself. All depends on why it is done. No act in and of itself is Christian—neither preaching, nor praying, nor speaking to men about Christ. It is made Christian by the motive. Is it done for love of Christ and the desire to live to the praise of his glory? Christians do many things that non-Christians do, but for different reasons. This makes the difference absolute.

A fifth reason is the dislike of stirring up trouble. The ministry of the cup of cold water evokes universal applause. Both recipient and spectators are pleased. But to take the part of the oppressed and exploited against the oppressor and exploiter is guaranteed to make some people "fightin' mad." By a strange misreading of the New Testament, many Christians take the position that nothing should ever be said or done which will disturb anybody. To do so, they feel, would be a denial of Christian love! So they never face issues within the fellowship of the church which might ruffle the deadly placidity of the most indifferent member; likewise, they never take a stand on any wrongdoing in society that might cause the slightest tremor among the forces of evil. They have forgotten the words of the greatest Disturber of all: "Woe unto you, when all men shall speak well of you! for so did their fathers to the *false prophets*" (Luke 6:26, italics mine). They have forgotten that their Lord was crucified because he refused to keep his mouth shut. They follow after—but so far in the rear that they have lost sight of the cross. It was these that Paul Scherer had in mind when he pictured the church as wandering "from room to room of humanity's tragic house, wringing its hands, mumbling its creeds, its best wishes and kindest regards, making its distant gestures toward eternity; not even meeting man's need, let alone shaping anything; apologizing for man's poverty; fawning on its governments at war; stroking a cross, but never getting itself crucified because it is not worth crucifying."[11]

There is a final reason for disapproving social education and action which is so important as to warrant more extended comment. It is a very widespread but nonetheless unbiblical view of spirituality. What I mean will be apparent when I give an illustration of how the Bible speaks at this point. In Leviticus 25, God makes provision for land reform among the Israelites. Every fifty years, any land belonging to the ancestral estate that had been sold was to be returned to the original owners. Indeed, the price attached to every sale of land was determined by the number of years that the buyer would have it for his use before he had to

[11] From *For We Have This Treasure,* by Paul Scherer (New York: Harper and Brothers. Copyright, 1944), p. 122. Used by permission.

give it back. The purpose of this legislation was to avoid the exploitation which would arise if big landlords acquired large amounts of land in perpetuity. The fiftieth year, the year in which the land was redistributed, was called the Year of Jubilee, and its arrival was to be proclaimed on the day of atonement (Lev. 25:9). The sixteenth chapter of Leviticus tells what the day of atonement was. It was that most holy day when the High Priest, entering into the Holy of Holies for the one and only time during the year, made atonement for the sins of the people. Note that this was the day when the program of land reform was to be announced, the Year of Jubilee!

The shock to the modern churchman is considerable. Imagine announcing a program for land reform at the equivalent of the Lord's supper! It appears to be a distressing breach of spirituality.

Now, what is it that separates the modern churchman from the spirit of Leviticus? It is the idea that the "spiritual" is a particular branch of life, a particular area of interest. So while statesmen deal with political things, artists with things like music and literature, and athletes with sports, churchmen deal with spiritual things (lead of course by the clergy, who are the experts in spiritual things, much as the economist is the expert in economics). Being spiritual is a form of specialized activity which includes helping the pastor run the church, working in the church, reading the Bible and praying. Then, after you have been especially spiritual on Sunday, you have to return on Monday to the non-spiritual world, to the work-a-day world, where you do the best you can to keep going until you can be spiritual again the next Sunday, as you share with your fellow Christians the joys of church life.

What is wrong with this picture? Certainly not the urge to worship, or to mingle with the brethren, or to read the

Bible and pray. Certainly not. What is wrong is conceiving of all these things as representing an area of concern isolated from the rest of the activities of life, an area that might roughly be called "church life," a sacred area as opposed to secular areas.

This is the twisted heresy that has come close to edging the churches right out of any living relations with the world of people round about it and into the monastery of irrelevance. This is the twisted heresy that can make it possible for Professor Commager to claim that the churches have never had so many members and at the same time so little influence in American life. This is the twisted heresy against which the Bible sets its face like a flint. This is the concept which our Lord refused to permit his disciples to adopt. How tempted they were to adopt it! When he finished preaching to the multitudes they were inclined to shrug off the food problem by saying, "You fed them with spiritual things; let them scrounge for their material things." But Jesus insisted, "Give ye them to eat" (Luke 9:13). When they ascended the Mount and the Lord was transfigured before them, Peter suggested that they build a church up there and "go spiritual"; but Jesus pointed them to the needs in the valley (Matt. 17). They were ready to make their experience an escape *from* reality; Jesus was determined that they should make it a door *to* reality.

The key to the understanding of the biblical idea of spirituality is to see what it is *not,* before trying to see what it is. The spiritual is not the opposite of the material. How could it be? "The earth is the Lord's, and the fulness thereof" (Ps. 24:1). The body is not the opposite of the soul. Not only was the body created by God, it is redeemed by God; and in that Great Day Coming we look forward, not to the immortality of the soul in a ghostly heaven, but to the resurrection of the body in a new heaven and a new earth (Rev.

21). Far from being the opposite of the spiritual, the material is the vehicle of it. Hence we proclaim the gospel of the Incarnation: "Wherefore when he cometh into the world, he saith, Sacrifice and offering thou wouldest not, but a body hast thou prepared me" (Heb. 10:5). The opposite of spirituality is not materiality but sin.

What then is spirituality? If we are to take seriously the idea that the Bible is the Word of God, and if our Lord has told us that the whole inner meaning and purpose of the Old Testament was love of God and love of neighbor, then we can only say that spirituality is love of God and love of neighbor; i.e., right interpersonal relations—first and primarily with God (conversion, redemption, prayer, worship, etc.) and then through God with the neighbor in loving service. The kingdom of God is the Kingdom of Right Relations. The church is the historical expression of this Kingdom of Right Relations. Wherever relations with God and man are wrong, whether it be within the church or out of it, there is sin. Whether it be called a race problem, or the problem of war and peace, or the problem of labor-management relations, or the family problem, or the problem of juvenile delinquency, there is sin. And where sin is, there the church has business to do. To the church has been given the ministry of reconciliation—of man with God and of man with his fellows. A ministry that is not reconciling is not the ministry given to the church by its Lord.

What this means for the church is that it must abandon its ghetto psychology and move out from behind its closed doors and stained-glass windows. As George MacLeod reminds us, our Lord "was not crucified in the cathedral between two candles, but in the market place between two thieves."[12] Furthermore, it is in the market place that we

[12] George MacLeod, *Only One Way Left* (Glasgow: Iona Press, 1958), p. 38. Used by permission.

meet our risen Lord. "He goeth before you." In the common experiences of our everyday lives the Word of God comes to us, claiming our obedience and offering us succor. "Ye are the light of the world," said our Lord. "Let your light shine."

The field is not the church, but the *world*. It is of the *world* that the statement is made that God so loved it that he gave his only begotton Son for it. It is for the *world*—of sinning, suffering, erring, laboring, dying men—that Christ died. And it is the *world* which has been given to the risen Christ for his inheritance. True, we are not *of* the world. Our standards, our insights, our goals, and our objectives reflect the heavenly homeland which we own. But though not *of* the world, we exist *for* the world. "As thou hast sent me into the world, even so have I also sent them into the world" (John 17:18). We are to be broken bread and poured out wine for its needs.

There are practical overtones for this truth in the deadly struggle of Christianity with Communism. Communism got its start and derives its strength from a ghetto Christianity. When Karl Marx said that religion was the opiate of the people, he meant that religion, by wrapping men's minds in the mists of otherworldliness, insulated men from the struggles and problems of our common life together in the world. When people say, "Let religion stay out of politics," "Let religion stay out of business," "Let religion stay out of everything but a little narrow corner of things which we will gladly assign to it"—when people say such things, they are giving voice to the Communist interpretation of the function of religion in society. To constrict the function of the Christian faith in the world in this fashion would fatally wound our witness and falsify the mission which we have been given. To this witness we must now turn.

THE CHURCH AS A WITNESSING COMMUNITY

The church is a witnessing community which exists for the evangelization of men. Gathered out of every tribe and nation, it points beyond itself to "the Lamb of God, which taketh away the sin of the world" (John 1:29). The church functions as the body of Christ and its only purpose is to make Christ known. The gospel is its precious possession, and in season and out of season it proclaims the gospel to an ignorant world. If the church is not a witnessing community, it is not a church. It is apostate, and henceforth is good for nothing but to be cast out and trodden under foot by the Communists, the intellectuals, and any others who may want to step on it. We must evangelize or perish from the face of the earth.

It is to the nature of the Christian witness, then, that we must now give attention. Our textbook will be the Book of Acts. In Chapter 1 the risen Lord tells his disciples that their responsibility is to be witnesses, but he forbids them to practice their vocation until they have waited and received the power to witness. So for several days, while men were going to hell all around them for lack of the truth, they "sat on" the biggest news story in history! They never said a word to anyone about the events which they had lived through.

At first, this seems very strange. After all, they had voices and apparently they were quite willing to use them in telling the story. But they were under the divine veto. They were not to talk to anyone—yet. What was the nature of this power which must precede performance? It was the power of God for which they waited. And God? He is love. Then the power for which they waited was the power to love. Without it they might be able to say words, even correct gospel words. But they really could not witness—not in a Christian sense.

Why not? To understand why not, we must realize that a witness may be any one of three kinds. He may be a spectator of events, who tells what he saw but did not participate in. Secondly, he may be related to the events to which he testifies, but in a peripheral way so that the events are not intimately connected with him—as when a passenger who himself got by without a scratch tells of the auto accident in which his fellow-passengers were permanently crippled. Finally, he may himself be one of the crippled passengers who, when he gives witness to the seriousness of the accident, is himself *part of the evidence* of that to which he bears witness.[13]

A Christian witness is one who is himself part of the evidence of that to which he testifies. (This is involved in what was said above, when it was stressed that we, as members of Christ's body, are part of the gospel which we preach.) For those early disciples, this meant that they were not permitted to speak the *words* of love until they had become the *community* of love and could do the *works* of love. Let us see if this squares with the facts as they are given us in Acts.

In Acts, Chapter 1, we find the disciples waiting. In Chapter 2, the "power from on high" comes, the love of God is shed abroad in their hearts through the Holy Ghost, and they are melted into one brotherhood. They all stand together—no bickering, no jealousy (Acts 2:14); they all speak together in unity about the wonderful works of God (Acts 2:11). They were drunk—with the love of Christ (Acts 2:13). That it was into a community of redeeming love that they were welded at Pentecost is shown by the

[13] I owe this illustration to Dr. D. T. Niles, who gave it in a public address.

first picture of the newly formed church (Acts 2:41-47). There they are shown as all being together, and having all things in common, and "continuing daily with one accord."

Now, in between that first picture of the church of the redeemed given at the end of the second chapter and the account of the coming of the Spirit given at the beginning of that second chapter is Peter's sermon. Peter got his chance to preach because people were amazed and began to ask questions about the meaning of this that had happened to the disciples. The content of Peter's preaching was an interpretation of what had happened in terms of the death and resurrection of Christ. First came the formation of the community, the church which is his body, and then the sermon interpreting the community.

Now turn to Chapter 3, the story of the healing of the lame man. Here the community of redeeming love is in action. Note that "Peter and John went up together" (Acts 3:1). Note also that "Peter, fastening his eyes upon him *with John,* said, Look on us" (Acts 3:4). When the man asked for a handout, Peter and John did not turn aside as did the priest and the Levite in the story of the Good Samaritan. Instead, they gave the man more than he asked. They performed the works of love. Seeing a man in bondage, they invoked for his release the Lordship of Jesus Christ over his world. Seeing a man in need, they invoked the love of Christ, focused and made available for the man's healing in their love for each other as well as for the man himself. "In the name of Jesus Christ of Nazareth," they said, "rise up and walk." Again the crowds came running. Again the astonishment and the questioning. Again the opportunity to interpret the meaning of what had been done by reference to the death and resurrection of Christ. So we have Peter's second gospel message (Acts 3:12-26).

Let me summarize and then draw my conclusions. In Acts 1, we have the injunction to the apostles to wait until the Holy Spirit makes something out of them and the consequent waiting. In Acts 2, the Holy Spirit forms the believers into the community of faith, hope, and love (2:1-13); Peter interprets this event in terms of the gospel (2:14-40); people are saved and gathered into the fellowship of believers, which is pictured as a unity-in-love (2:41-47). In Acts 3, this fellowship of believers, this unified-in-the-love-of-Christ community, performs the works of love representatively in the persons of Peter and John (3:1-11); Peter then interprets what has been done in terms of the gospel (3:12-26). In Acts 4, this good deed brings upon them persecution (4:1-22), which only serves to bind the Christian fellowship closer together in love and prayer (4:23-32), which in turn increases the power of their witness (4:33), which binds them together all the closer in love (4:34-37). In Acts 5, we read that a deception, unfortunately, disrupts the unity of the brotherhood, but the health of the Body is such that it throws off the infection in an awesome fashion (5:1-11). Meanwhile, by the hand of the apostles, many signs and wonders are done (5:12).

What is God trying to tell us in all this? The answer marks the end of some of our most cherished and damaging prejudices and the beginning—God grant—of a new understanding of the biblical meaning of witness. Witness cannot be carried by words alone. If it is the love of Christ to which we would witness, we must *become* the love of Christ in incarnation and effectual deed in order to speak meaningfully of it. Love must be in the present tense to be significant. "You were loved by Christ two thousand years ago" is poor comfort for needy persons today. But when the world sees the love of Christ incarnate in the church and in action in the world, then the claims of God's love in Christ become relevant. The church is a sign of the resurrection of Love from the dead and of Love's present overruling, releasing power.

The ideal order of witness is clear from these early pages of Acts. The church first exists as the community of love, then it does the work of love, and then it speaks—and its words are weighty words because they are interpretative. They relate what the church is and does, to the death and resurrection of Jesus Christ and his exaltation to lordship. Not that this order has to be maintained by every individual. It would be quite intolerable if I were never permitted to say anything to a passing stranger by way of witness because I had not first had opportunity of doing something for him. Even Paul sometimes did nothing but speak, because there was no opportunity to do otherwise. But the truth we have been tracing nevertheless remains sure. Unless in the over-all witness of the church, it first reveals love in its fellowship and then in its actions, its words will fall as in a vacuum. First *be*, then *do*, then *say*. This is the divine order. Christian witness, in its fullness, is the name for all three of these movements—being, doing, and talking—in their interrelations.

It now becomes clear that I have been writing about witnessing all along in this chapter and not under this last heading only. When the church is a mothering community in which men are bound together in Christian love, the church *is* a witness. Our Lord clearly said so. "By this," he said, "shall all men know that ye are my disciples, if we have love one to another" (John 13:35). Not by what you say, but by the love of Christ bodied forth in the fellowship of the Christian church, are you known and recognized. Again, Jesus prays ". . . that they all may be one; as thou,

Father, art in me, and I in thee, that they also may be one in us: *that the world may believe that thou hast sent me"* (John 17:21). The church is the reflection on earth of the unity-in-diversity of the Trinity. The world believes in Jesus' divine mission when it sees the supernatural love of Christ at work in the unity-in-love of the brethren.

This is why a church which segregates the races and Jim Crows the body and blood of our Lord Jesus Christ at the Communion Table is a blasphemous church (where "blasphemy" is defined as intentionally offering indignity to the Supreme Being). The "for-whites-only" church advertises to the world that all its talk about "Christ is the answer" is a sham. It is saying, in effect, that its members have Christ, and that they love their fellow believers of different skin with such a supernatural love that they will not even let them into their church that they may worship their common Lord together! Their vaunted claim to redemption-into-love is shown to be empty, and the world scoffs, just as our Lord said by indirection that it would.

I am not talking here about a social problem. I am talking about an evangelistic problem. A missionary friend of mine in Indonesia says that instead of evangelizing, he has to spend half his time trying to explain why American Christians have the racial attitudes they do. My own experience is similar. In 1953 a young Brazilian came half way across the city of Rio to discuss Christ with me. An unbeliever, he had a philosophical background and had been sent to me for that reason. His question was simple and it was not philosophical. "I only want to ask you one thing," he said. "Why do white Christians in America treat the Negroes the way they do? I shouldn't think that would be Christian."

Paul said that in Christ there are no racial distinctions, no class distinctions, no sex distinctions, but a unity-in-love (Gal. 3:28). When the power of the love of Christ to melt down all human divisions and to create a new unity is denied in practice, the truth of the gospel is thereby denied and no verbal assertion of the gospel's truth, however orthodox, can redress the matter. Yesterday's evangelists got the point. In their "protracted meetings" they tried to get the churches right with God before they preached to sinners. It is hard to preach the gospel when you have no evidence to appeal to!

But when the church operates as a ministering community, it is raising its witness too. Just as our Lord said that people would not be impressed by our words but would be impressed by our willingness to love one another, so he said similarly that people would not glorify God because of our talk but only because of our deeds. "Ye are the light of the world. . . . Let your light so shine before men, that they may *hear your good talk.*" No, that is the *modern* translation. Permit me to begin again: "Ye are the light of the world. . . . Let your light so shine before men, that they may see your good works, and glorify your Father which is in heaven" (Matt. 5:14-16). Good works are a witness, says our Lord. 1 Peter repeats it (1 Pet. 2:12). The healing of the lame man at the Gate Beautiful illustrates it, for we read that "all men glorified God for that which was done" (Acts 4:21). How could it have been otherwise? God is a worker, not a talker. It is not advice that Christ is famous for, but a sacrifice. We preach not the wonderful *words* of God, but the wonderful *works* of God. If this is true, the weight of the witness cannot be carried by words only. The God who did the Deed of love can be interpreted adequately only by deeds of love. It is that simple. But where is there a church whose program is organized around this truth? Where are the evangelizing deeds?[14]

Now that we have seen that the church, speaking biblically, is a ministering community, and is by that very fact a witnessing community (assuming that its motive is right, and its heart is right toward God), we are ready to look again at the various kinds of ministering deeds to which we made reference earlier. A new centrality is thereby established for the second kind—the on-the-job ministry. Working for Christ in our leisure time is fine and important. But we spend more time in working for a living than we do in leisure-time activities, and it is in our occupational life that we most obviously and immediately make our impress upon the world to whom we are sent by our Lord. At the point of our jobs, we cannot avoid the world of men and things, nor can they avoid us. Here then, a primary witness is raised for good or for ill; namely, in and through the job itself. Here is the scattered church—scattered abroad to testify of God's grace and redeeming strength. Wherever the Christian is—in the factory, in the office, in the field, on the road, in the labor union, in the government—there the church of Jesus Christ representatively is bearing its witness to the realities of the changed life in Christ by the way in which the job is done, the situations are met, and the tensions are handled, as well as by the words which are used (and not used) and the ideas discussed. This is why there is great hope for evangelism in the slowly (all too slowly) emerging practice of getting together men and women from the same vocational groups to face together in interchange of ideas what it means to be a Christian in their kind of job.

[14] It is a measure of our perversion of New Testament truth that it can be assumed as most probable that the majority of readers, on reading that last sentence, will immediately react to the term "evangelizing deeds" in accordance with their first impression, which is to the effect that it refers to sending teams of *talkers* into the community.

One man who attended his first retreat of this sort remarked that it was the first time in forty years of church attendance that he had heard anything that helped him in his occupational problem. (He was excepting, of course, the frequently heard simple generalities, such as "Be kind" and "Be good.")

A young man, unsaved, though a product of a Christian home and Sunday school, signed up for summer work on the staff of a denominational assembly. His first week brought him his first crisis. Pushing a cart loaded with dishes through the kitchen, he upset and ruined the cook's newly baked cake. Now this cook's most famous product was his cake. It was what he liked to do best and prided himself on most. The young man knew this, and seeing the shambles, he braced himself for the storm. It never came. Instead, the cook said quietly: "Never mind. We'll bake another." Speaking of the episode years later, the young man testified, "That was the first time that I ever saw anything appealing in Christianity." A Christian was on the job for Christ, while on his job!

What of that other rather controversial form of ministering which we discussed—the ministry of social action? That, too, is a form of witness. To see it as such is to bypass a raft of questions that really do not greatly matter, as far as our motivation is concerned. Questions like: "What good will it do to try to reform things?" "What hope do we have of achieving a warless world?" "Why waste our energy writing our Senator; we're taking a minority position that can't win." And, "Why indulge in social action when we know that the kingdom of God won't really come until Christ returns?" These are not unimportant questions when it comes to seeing social action in the total perspective of Christian truth. They raise the big question of what the church can hope for in society. Has it the right to hope for complete social success? or must it expect steady failure until Christ's return? or is the truth somewhere in between?

My point is not that such questions are unimportant, but rather that they are not relevant to the *basic* question, "Must we engage in social action?" That question is answered when we see that, quite aside from the consequences, Christian social action is a necessity as a part of the witness of the ministering community, the church. Philippe Maury says it wonderfully well when he writes: "The Christian in politics [and we may add, any other form of social action— C. G. R.] will give himself wholly to the action in which he is engaged, yet remain skeptical about what he is doing. Success is not indispensable, because his final hope is not political but in the glory of God. Political action should be a means of making clear the meaning of faith in Christ."[15] Wonderful! Christian social action is a form of witness to the love and lordship of Christ. It is a way of living for the praise of his glory.

Incidentally, this is a totally different thing than living for the collection of statistics. A church that in a burst of zeal engages in a ministry of service only to abandon it when it sees no increase in "conversions and decisions" has missed the point entirely. Loving people only as long as we think they are prospects for church membership is not to love them at all. Witnessing to them only as long as we think there is a chance of our deriving some benefit can be a very subtle form of self-aggrandizement. We have no mandate to cease witnessing to the world merely because the witness is not received the way we think it should be. We forget that one soweth and another reapeth. Christ himself is, after all, the evangelist. We are but witnesses—part of the evidence.

[15] Quoted in *The Christian Century,* March 16, 1949, p. 347. Used by permission.

Yet, after sounding this warning, it is altogether appropriate to illustrate the connection between social action and evangelism by telling a "success story." Here it is, as told by the man to whom it happened, Dr. Len Broughton, founder of the famous Baptist Tabernacle in Atlanta, Georgia, to Dr. W. W. Adams, after the latter had been hammering away at a group of ministers with some of the same truths that I have been pleading for in this chapter.[16] The time was August in the early 1920's; the place Atlanta. Typhoid fever had broken out in a small area which had recently been incorporated within the city limits, but to which, as yet, city services had not been extended. Four people had died, due to the typhoid germs found in the water. This got in the headlines, was talked about, but nothing was done. Saturday the city authorities met, discussed it, but did nothing. At the same meeting, $15,000 was voted to pave the street in front of the house of one of the big city politicians who knew how to pull wires.

This was too much for Dr. Broughton. He called up the authorities and said: "I want two of your men in my church tomorrow morning."

It came time to read the Scripture. He said, "You have come (there was a large audience) to hear me preach on the advertised topic. I am asking you to let me keep that till next Sunday." With that, he spelled out the situation in the city and said, "I want to show you the Word of God." For fifty minutes he opened up the Bible, showing how God, who had made all things, including our bodies as well as

[16] If it sounds somewhat as though I were dragging in the name of Dr. W. W. Adams, I am. It gives me opportunity to say that it was he, as my New Testament professor in seminary, who taught me to read the Bible with open eyes. This story is taken from the stenographically reported notes of an address which he gave at the Christian Life Workshop held in Fort Worth, Texas, Feb. 9, 1959.

our spirits, wants us to live fully, wholly, and completely. He is just as eager for people to have good water to drink as to have them go to prayer meeting. Before Broughton was half through, the two men from City Hall were trying to hide behind the people in front of them.

When the benediction was over Dr. Broughton stepped down in front and for one hour people gripped his hand, some with tears, as they thanked him for speaking for God and for them. But that is not the point. The next morning before ten o'clock the money was voted by the city authorities and in thirty-six hours the epidemic was stopped. But even that is not the point. Here it is: In the next three months he baptized over seventy-five people, almost all of whom told him that they first became interested in his church and his Christ because he had helped those people get good water to drink.

"Let your light so shine . . . ," unless you are lacking in courage.

This chapter is already too long. Yet I am loath to close it without first underscoring some of the implications of the preceding analysis.

CONCLUSION NUMBER ONE: A rethinking of the meaning of evangelism is called for. Evangelism is the proclamation in word, deed, and fellowship-life of God's saving will and energy in Jesus Christ. The adoption of some such formula would bring an end to the church's obsession with word-magic. It is a matter of some astonishment to note how completely a trust in words dominates the modern church. Organization pyramids on organization, all working with the same formula: a corps of officers and a program of meetings, with the end in view of having the members properly talked to. Ansel Gibbs, the hero of Fred Buech-

ner's novel *The Return of Ansel Gibbs,* writes his daughter:
"I have been at a loss for everything else perhaps, but never
for words. I was made for words. I sometimes believe that
I am made of words."[17] The world believes this of the
church.

CONCLUSION NUMBER TWO: A radical overhaul of the
church's image of itself is long overdue—and the laity must
spark it. The average overworked minister finds himself
called to a church whose pattern and program is, within
limits, already well set. Just to run in the well-worn grooves
takes almost all his energy. So long as the laity keep him
working overtime in the already established pattern of activities, he is not likely to dream up new ways of keeping
busy. The fact of the matter is that much—perhaps most—
of what goes on in the local church should be scuttled.
Every organization should be forced to justify its existence
in the light of the church's mandate from its Lord. But most
of all, the preacher-centered church should be transformed.
The church must see itself as primarily a ministering community, not a talked-at congregation. The pastor's prime
responsibility is so to preach and train his laity that they will
become preachers in turn—preachers of the gospel by their
lives, deeds, and words out in the world. The church im-
pinges on the life of the world, *not* in its pastor, but in its
laity. The work and witness of the believing church is
inevitably the work and witness of the membership. This
is the meaning of the doctrine of the priesthood of all
believers. A priest has access to God; this side of the priesthood of all believers is well known among Protestants. But
a priest also represents God before men; this other side of
the priesthood of all believers is completely ignored. If all

[17] From *The Return of Ansel Gibbs,* by Fred Buechner (New York:
Alfred A. Knopf, Inc., Copyright, 1958). Used by permission.

believers are priests, then the pastor has no more ultimate responsibility for getting the gospel out than the most humble layman. It is a membership job.[18]

CONCLUSION NUMBER THREE: The term "social implications of the gospel" should be abandoned. If the above-argued view of the gospel is correct, they are not social implications but social imperatives. Again, if the above-argued view of the gospel is correct, social action has its honored place among the ways of getting the gospel out into the world. Even more, if the church really is itself part of the gospel, then its ministry of deeds—including social deeds—is part of the gospel's good news to men. This change of terminology is not just a whim. It is important if the issue is to be met head on. The word "implications" permits the average church to think of this form of witness as something it can get around to if it has time; it allows the church to regard it as good, but peripheral. The center of the church's interest, on this interpretation, obviously is in the other things to which the church gives its attention. In this way, the pressure of these other things can keep the church *permanently* dodging this form of witness with a good conscience, and permits the denomination year after year to starve the Council on Christian Social Progress with an all-but-invisible budget.

This whole chapter is an effort to bury the kind of thinking which makes evangelism the thing and social action only an implication. On my view—which I believe to be biblical —social action *is* evangelism in one of its important forms. Evangelism is the broad term which includes within its scope the witness of the church through social action. In-

---

[18] A church would be well advised to call its whole membership together for the Wednesday nights of the winter for studying, praying, and planning as to how to become a ministering community. It should analyze the needs of its area and look at ways by which these needs might be met.

deed, social action becomes mere do-goodism when it is divorced from a warm passion for the souls of men and the cause of Christ. On the other hand, evangelism deteriorates easily into escapism and mere talk when it is divorced from a warm and genuine social passion in Christ's name.

4

THE CHRIST WHO WILL BE

"FAITH, HOPE, AND LOVE." These are the great words of the Christian life. We have seen something of what it means for the church to be a community of faith in Jesus Christ and of love toward Christ and neighbor. We must now look at the church as a community of hope, for hope too is related to Jesus Christ. We are saved in hope. The Christ who was and is, becomes also the Christ who will be. The gospel is not preached in its fullness without this future look. In the preaching of the gospel there is always a note of expectancy: "Stay tuned to this station for future developments." There definitely will be "future developments."

Not that the church knows what all the future developments will be. It does not, for no one can read God's mind. The church knows only what has been given to it to know; and what has been given to it to know is not the process itself but the end of the process, not the steps but where the steps lead to. In short, the church knows where things are going, but it does not know the details of how they are going to get there. The church is one of the actors in the great drama called "History." Nobody has ever showed it the script, so it has to play its part by ear, according to the whispered instructions of the Great Prompter. But it knows what the general theme is, and, best of all, it knows how the whole play ends. It has been given a peek at the last scene.

The idea that history is moving toward a destined end, that there is a meaning and purpose in it, is a biblical idea. It has become secularized and wedded to the idea of evolutionary progress in modern times, but it was the Bible which first taught the human race to think in terms of a purpose in history. Berdaiev, the famous Russian student of history, says that the first book in the history of the world which sought to spell out the direction of the story was the Book of Daniel. Indeed the very idea that history *has* a direction is a biblical idea. To the Greeks, as well as to the great religious teachers of the Orient, history had no direction. Salvation consisted in turning one's back on history and seeking what lay behind history. But the Christ-faith, as we saw in the first chapter, is a historical religion. It derives its nourishment and strength from an Event in history, and it stays tied to history all the way, because it knows that God is working out his purposes in history. The human story is not aimless. God has a hand in it. He has a hand in it for good.

To see the way that the Christian understands history, one must see it as the struggle between God and rebellious man. History is the story of this struggle, the struggle between good and evil. It sometimes looks as though evil were going to win, but that is an illusion. God still reigns. Then why does not God do something? He has and does. But God has to work within the rules of the game that he started when he made man in his own image. That is to say, God has to put down evil in a way that does not override or deny the freedom of man. Of course, God could light a match to the whole thing and let it all go up in smoke. This would get rid of the villains—the leaders of evil, the oppressors of the race. It would also get rid of us. What is more, it would also be an admission that the whole idea of creating in the first place was a mistake.

No, God's ways are not our ways nor are his thoughts our thoughts. God works through a Man and a Cross, and he works successfully. The great good news of the gospel includes the word that evil will be cast out of God's universe and that a redeemed race will enter into God's inheritance.

Well . . . it makes a nice story, happy ending and all. But what is the evidence? This struggle between good and evil has been going on since the dawn of recorded time and it gives no sign of abating. The gospel of Jesus Christ is here and has been preached for two thousand years, and still the struggle goes on. Nothing happens. Nothing. What is the evidence that it is not all a pipe dream, this business of a happy ending? Indeed, what is the evidence that history is going *anywhere?* Maybe this see-saw battle of good with evil is all there is—a meaningless struggle to squeeze purpose out of a purposeless, indifferent universe. Maybe the end of it is the extinction of all life on the earth, human as well as subhuman, while the earth like a burned-out cinder or perhaps like a frozen iceberg moves meaning-lessly and lifelessly through space, its brief experiment with that frustrated, frustrating, maddening creature, Man, for-ever ended.

If our generation feels puzzled at the persistence of evil and its continuing power, it is not the first generation to feel that way. Indeed, the modern mood could be dupli-cated almost to the letter by the mood of the Jews of Jesus' day. They too were the heirs of promises of a better day. Throughout their history they had believed that they were a chosen race with a great destiny. In moments of grave peril and crisis, their prophets had thundered the judgments of God, but they had always added the promise of God to bring the messianic reign: "There will be a Day. . . ." "A Day is going to come. . . ." But it never came. Foreign nations overran the country. Ten of the twelve tribes of Israel went into captivity and never came back. The little kingdom of Judah never had a chance. Sometimes Judah was independent, but by and large she became the pawn of larger powers in their struggle for dominion. She was up and down, up and down, century after century. The promises of the prophets of God remained . . . promises. Nothing happened. Nothing.

Then, suddenly, it looked as though something *was* happening. A Man appeared who cried, "The Time is at hand." This was different. Throughout their history the cry always had been, "It shall come to pass." But here was One saying, "The Time is fulfilled. The Kingdom is here. Repent and believe." And people did believe. For two, three years, things hummed: the dead were raised, the blind were given sight, the lame were made to walk, the truth was proclaimed as it had never been proclaimed before. The disciples, at least, were sure that here was he who was to deliver Israel. But finally the forces of the opposition that he had challenged so magnificently got to him through the twisted personality of one of his own inner circle. He was betrayed—and that ended that. As he was dying, the crowd reminded him of his fine words and promised to believe in him if he would make the nails drop out of his hands and feet and would step down off the cross. For one wild moment the disciples thought maybe he would. But he did not do so. Nothing happened. Nothing. Disillusionment was never more complete.

One will never really get the "feel" of the gospel unless one sees how easily the crucifixion of Christ could make an atheist of one. Here was sheer goodness—crucified. Jesus was young, idealistic, eager. He prayed constantly and trusted God implicitly. If he had lived to a normal age, he could have done much good in the world, but he died before he really got started. Injustice proved stronger than justice;

hate proved stronger than love; badness proved stronger than goodness. And God? "Surely," men said, "there is no God." In a world where Jesus Christ gets crucified and the Pilates and the Caiaphases sit on top of the heap, one can only speak of the supreme indifference of the universe to all our strivings and values. The cross has a message all right. It seems to say, "There is no God."

This is one way, and a very understandable way, of interpreting the cross. Yet it is in connection with the cross where the problem of evil is raised in its most acute form and where all the difficulties that have troubled men concerning the course of history are focused most sharply, that the Christian speaks of the revelation of the mercy and love of God. The Christian faith does not dodge the problem of evil. When it makes the cross its living center, it meets the problem head-on.

But how can Christian faith speak in this way? How can what looks like atheism be turned around to serve as evidence for the very opposite? The answer is, the resurrection. At the resurrection, everything fell into place and made sense. The disciples had not been wrong, after all, about Christ. It was merely that God's plans and purposes and strategy were bigger than anything that they had dreamed of. They had been cut in on the inconceivably mighty work of the Omnipotent and Eternal One.

The resurrection meant recognition. Many years ago, I am told, the mayor of Boston decided during a hard and difficult winter to learn at first hand about the sufferings of the poor. He disguised himself as a down-on-his-luck derelict, and ended up by chopping wood for his supper at the Salvation Army. Chopping wood was a new experience, and although his hands became raw and tired, his strokes continued to be ineffectual. A fellow derelict took pity on him, took the axe from his hand, and cut up all his allotted wood.

In a burst of gratitude, the mayor whipped out his card and told the man that if he would come to the mayor's office the following Monday he would get him a job. The man passed it off as the delusion of a sick but harmless fellow. But Monday, drawn by a mixture of motives, including curiosity, the derelict showed up at the appointed time. His jaw dropped. There across the desk was the man for whom he had done the good deed the preceding week. His fellow derelict was the mayor of Boston.

The resurrection produced just such a recognition scene. Calvary's weak and helpless victim proved to be God's Man of the Hour. God had not been absent at the tragedy of Calvary; indeed, never had God been more present in the affairs of men. The friendless and unresisting man whom wicked hands had slain was the Prince of Heaven, the Lord from Glory.

Recognition meant vindication. The grain of the universe ran in Christ's direction, not Herod's nor Caiaphas'. The things for which Christ stood, the truths of which he spoke, the love which he demonstrated—these were the enduring, living, powerful realities of the world; not the lust, the power-drive, the hate, the selfishness, the sin of men and nations. God's guarantee stood back of Christ's kind of life. He was right, forever right.

But in one sense the vindication was incomplete. The risen Christ came only to the disciples. His enemies neither saw his resurrection nor did they believe the apostolic witness to it, though the disciples proclaimed it boldly and faithfully in the very city where six weeks before their master had been put to death. To the early believers the resurrection was everything. It created a new day (Sunday), a new book (the New Testament), and a new community (the church). But to the unbelieving world the resurrection said nothing. To them, it did not exist. All continued the same. Success still belonged to the clever, the conniving, the selfish, the powerful, and the compromising.

Hence, for the vindication of Jesus Christ something else was needed. What was hidden must become manifest for all the world to see. What only the heart of faith then knew must become known to all. Every eye must see; every knee must bow; every tongue must confess. The lordship of Christ must become a universally recognized fact.

What the logic of vindication demanded, the good of the world also demanded. The world would never be right until it was ruled by Jesus Christ. He and he alone could handle the problem of power over the lives and destinies of men. Power in the hands of the Herods, the Caiaphases, or the Caesars is a corrupting influence. Only one man lived with power and was not corrupted by it, even in the slightest, and that was Jesus Christ. He held more power in his hand than was held by any other man who ever lived. He wielded the power of God over the powers of darkness. Disease fled at his touch. The demons of darkness quailed in his presence. At his word the dead rose. He could have commanded legions of angels (Matt. 26:53). But he never abused power or misused it. He never employed it for his own selfish ends, but only for the good of others. In him power was yoked to self-giving love. In him power was wedded to meekness and humility. He alone is good enough to rule the lives of men.

What his vindication demanded and the well-being of the world cried for, the will of God has assured. God has promised to reconcile and unify all things in Christ, both in heaven and on earth (Eph. 1:9-10; Col. 1:20). For this consummation the church waits. It looks for the return of its Lord in triumph and glory. Then every knee shall bow and every tongue shall confess, for the word of the Lord has spoken it (Phil. 2:10-11). What God will yet do in and through Jesus Christ—this too is part of the good news of the gospel of God.

I do not mean to imply that as soon as the disciples were confronted by the Risen Lord, all these ideas popped immediately into their heads. They did not. But as time went on, the early Christian community did come to think in this way. The key to their understanding was the resurrection. In the light of it (and the ascension and exaltation of our Lord which stemmed from it), they got a bird's-eye view of the whole sweep of history that was something like the following:

In the beginning God created. But sin marred the creation. God bestirred himself and set out to put things straight. He elected a people for his name and established a covenant with them at Mt. Sinai whereby they would be his people and he would be their God. His election of them was for service and humble usefulness, in pursuance of his revealed purpose as early as Abraham, to whom he had declared: "I will make of thee a great nation . . . and thou shalt be a great blessing . . . and in thee shall all families of the earth be blessed" (Gen. 12:2-3). But the Covenant People had not seen it that way. Election to them meant being blessed, not being a blessing. They became proud of their spiritual status and selfish in their hearts. God accordingly delivered them over to their enemies, but rescued them from time to time as repentance set in.

It then became apparent that the nation was too mixed a multitude to serve as God's instrument for blessing, and the hope for the future became lodged in a Remnant who would perform the vocation of the Suffering Servant of God. But the Remnant proved unequal to the task, until the day when the Remnant was narrowed down to one Representative Man. In his own person, he became the Suffering Servant. Through him the purposes of God were fulfilled. So, because he was obedient unto death, he has been exalted to be God's righthand man, the Lord of history (cf. Phil. 2:5-11). By him and in him a new covenant is formed, a new remnant is established, which is called the Church of the Suffering Servant, and which is identified with him in his ministry of salvation. This new Chosen People are, again, the elect of God—which means they have been chosen to serve and suffer for his name. They work and they witness to a Salvation already effected, to a Victory already won, to a Lord already enthroned. Meanwhile, the Lord works through them and outside of them, in ways beyond their knowing, until the work of his hidden Lordship is complete and the moment of unveiling or manifestation has arrived.

I use the term "unveiling" or "manifestation" advisedly. It is the more usual New Testament term for what is also referred to as the return of Christ. I prefer the term "unveiling," because it prevents us from thinking that our Lord is off somewhere on Cloud No. 9 in some distant galaxy, some hundreds of thousands of light years away. The spiritual world and the material world are not so related. On the contrary, the spiritual world surrounds, sustains, envelopes, and penetrates the material world at every moment. The trouble is that we are too materialistic, too time-bound, too sinful to take notice. But there are times when the curtain that divides the spiritual world from our material world rubs thin and we can "see through" and know that we live and move and have our being in God. In such moments our Lord is, in all truth, "closer than breathing, nearer than hands or feet." From the spirit world, he rules and guides the processes of history—until The Moment, that moment for which not only the church but also the whole creation waits. The veil which hides the realities of the spirit world from our eyes will then be rent. Eternity will come crashing into time, shattering the structures of history, and God's

New Order will begin. The instrument of this crashing in is Jesus Christ himself, who thereby is manifested as God's appointed Sovereign and Ruler of mankind, the one who has been "calling the plays" and working out the strategy all the time.

I have purposely avoided all reference to the millennium. The scriptural passages involved are full of pitfalls for the unwary and the experts are not all agreed. One can live a happy, effective Christian life and believe in a literal millennium and one can live a happy, effective Christian life and "spiritualize" these passages. Furthermore, it is neither healthy nor wise to be overly curious about the details of God's future plans. Let us be satisfied with what is clear and trust the rest to God. What *is* clear is that we can look forward to a new heaven and a new earth in which righteousness dwells (Rev. 21). This is the last picture drawn in the New Testament. It is a picture of a redeemed humanity, living with God and with one another in peace and prosperity. Not only is humanity redeemed, but also the whole universe has been purged and transformed as a fit habitation for the redeemed of God. As Bishop Aulén has put it: "Faith is compelled to look forward to the accomplishment of God's perfect dominion as being effected by a radical transformation and re-creation of things as they are."[1] Man and his whole environment are transformed and made new as eternity dawns.

We must not lose the significance of this final picture of human blessedness by reducing it to the trivial or the boring. Eternity is not monotonous timelessness. Rather, it is time fulfilled. Edwyn Bevan has suggested that time is the form of God's working, eternity the form of God's rest. He rests, not in the sense that there is nothing to do but sit around all day, but rather in the sense that there are no more

[1] From *The Faith of the Christian Church,* by Gustaf Aulén (Philadelphia: Muhlenberg Press, Copyright, 1948), p. 445. Used by permission.

enemies to be put down, no more conflicts to be resolved, no more imperfections to be dealt with, no more sin, no more suffering, and no more death. All the travail of history lies behind and God is all and in all. Time is measured by imperfection; eternity by perfection. Time is the period of the incomplete; eternity, of the complete. Time is "en route"; eternity is arrival. Eternity involves activity, but then there is no more sand in the carburetor, no more friction in the gears. Everything and everybody meshes perfectly together without strain or breakdown. Eternity is the world of Dreams Come True. It is not the End, except insofar as it is the end of the nightmare of human history with its sorrows, sufferings, death, wars, injustices, and bloodshed. Eternity is the Beginning. Henceforth all the redeemed live in complete fullness of life. A brand new chapter of God's dealing with his people opens. Indeed, if the term did not mislead, we might say that a new kind of history begins.

The link between the old order and God's New Order is Jesus Christ himself. Once he appeared, the humiliated one, to bear the sins of many. Once more he will appear, the glorified one, to bring to completion the revelation and redemption which he effected at such cost on Calvary's tree.

Jesus Christ is the inescapable one. This is what gives to life and our human story such seriousness. As Kierkegaard puts it, it is the Pattern that says, "I will come again." This is an ominous thought or a joyous thought, according to what a man's relation to the Pattern has been. For to say that the *Pattern* will come again is to say that life-as-I-live-it must one day answer to life-as-it-ought-to-be-lived. This is judgment in the sense of verdict. That is to say, every life will be exposed for what it actually is in the light of the Standard, not for what it is able to fool people into thinking that it is. This is the separation of the wicked from the righteous (righteous by God's grace only). This is the division of those who are with God from those who are against God. This is the manifestation of the truth that the wages of sin is death but the gift of God is eternal life. This is the revelation of the deadly seriousness of our choices and decisions. They are choices and decisions not only for time but also for eternity.

The generation which happens to be living at The Moment must answer for good or ill for its choices, but not that generation only. That would be most unjust. Rather, everybody is brought back onto the stage for the grand finale. Everybody receives the verdict, for life or death. This is resurrection.

I am not sure how good an analogy it is (and if it is not helpful, forget it), but I like to think of the relation between the old order and the new that is yet to come as not unlike the relation between the egg and the life of the hatched chick. In the dark womb of history, God is preparing something which is destined to break out into eternity. All that is of God in history is "hatched" into that eternal order. Nothing that was done or attempted for God is lost or wasted. Whatever in history is not of God is lost and discarded. It is important to see that the egg stage is not the final one; there is something yet to come that is greater than the life which is hidden in the egg could possibly comprehend.

We seem to have left the early disciples way behind in all this talk about eternity. But it only seems so. In actuality, for them as for us, the key to the future is supplied by the resurrection of Jesus Christ from the dead. They came to see that in Christ, Tomorrow had walked into today. Jesus Christ was the Future, and God had inserted the Future into their own times and they had seen and touched and handled—and believed. History was moving toward Christ, not chaos. Tomorrow would bring them—Christ. They themselves would become like him, for they would see him as he really is (1 John 3:2). Christ was the head of a new humanity which would inherit the earth. The resurrection was the pledge and assurance that all this would come to pass. Why? Because the resurrection showed that nothing could stop the onward sweep of Christ. In him a power was loose in the world, a power stronger than all the forces that opposed him. Herod, Caiaphas, Pilate, Caesar, corrupt religion, all-powerful government, the structures of society, sin, hell, and death—he had proved himself stronger than all of them. Nothing could stop him now.

If the resurrection was the pledge of the future, Pentecost was the confirmation of that future. In Christ they had seen the future shining in their own present. Eternity had walked into time. But in the coming of the Holy Spirit with resurrection power, the future had actually entered into them. Eternity had walked into their own purged and forgiven lives. Wonder of wonders, they had now been grasped by the powers of the world to come. They had already, here and now, tasted the realities of God's New Order!

It is this element of confirmation that is so strongly emphasized in Peter's sermon at Pentecost (Acts 2:14-36). The risen Christ had assured them that when he left them he would be headed for the power-center of the universe. When they were immersed in the Holy Spirit, they knew that he had arrived (Acts 2:33). This was the agreed-on signal. From then on, things would be different. There was a Man in the heavenlies.

Thus was born the community of resurrection, the community of hope. The word "hope," as used here, must be clearly understood. It is not the same as "wish." Their hoping was not a mere wishing. It was more. It was a promised fulfillment, of which the resurrection was a face-to-face pledge, of something already set up in history and already sampled in their lives. Behind the promised future stood the character of God himself. They could not lose. They were riding the wave of the future.

The community of resurrection was a community of hope precisely because it both possessed and did not possess. It possessed revelation, but in an incomplete form which would not be complete until God's Tomorrow. Thus Paul says, "For now we see through a glass, darkly; but then face to face. Now I know in part; but then shall I know even as also I am known" (1 Cor. 13:12). Similarly, it possessed redemption. Eternal life (the life of resurrection) was a present possession, but in an incomplete form. Its fullness awaited the coming in triumph of the Man from heaven.

Thus the church (and, of course, all that I have said about the early church is true of the church in each succeeding generation) is a unique and somewhat puzzling fellowship. It belongs, definitely, to Tomorrow; but it is also a part of today. It knows Tomorrow, it lives by the power of Tomorrow, it is the community of Tomorrow, but always in an incomplete way, because Tomorrow is not yet here and it is surrounded by today, with all its temptations, struggles, hardships, and heartaches. As Norman Grubb has expressed it, we are "in the flesh but not of it, in the world but not of it, and in self but not of it."[2] In short, we live by faith and not by sight. Salvation is our most priceless possession and at the same time our most longed for aspiration.

All of this is of great practical importance. It puts a limit on what a person has a right to expect from the Christian faith in this life. Sometimes, in presenting the gospel, we make the appeal that "it works." This is a legitimate appeal, if we make clear what is meant by the claim "it

[2] From *The Deep Things of God,* by Norman Grubb (London: Lutterworth Press, 1958), p. 45. Used by permission.

works." What can we expect in consequence of our meeting with Jesus Christ as Savior and Lord? Misunderstanding here is frequent. Take Carrie Ten Boom. During World War II she was arrested and placed in a Dutch concentration camp. She prayed and prayed that she would not be shipped off by the Nazis to Germany. But she *was* sent by the Nazis to Germany. Did her Christianity work? Not if by "working" you mean that her prayers would be answered and she would be allowed to stay in Holland. Then it did not work. But the story is not finished. God had a task for her to do. She took her Bible with her to the German concentration camp, and by God's grace she promoted a small but effective revival among the other prisoners. It all depends on what you mean by "it works."

Some new converts seem greatly surprised to find that life does not become for them a bed of roses. They expected to be without a care in the world; they anticipated that all their wishes would be met and that every dream would come true. When things do not turn out that way, they pout and complain that they are losing their faith. Apparently they conceived of God as a cosmic Sugar Daddy who would give them all their little hearts desired. It cannot be stressed too strongly that this dreams-come-true experience belongs to God's New Order, not to this present one. Christianity is not a means of avoiding the sufferings of life, or of building a more successful business, or of making the capitalistic system work better, or of saving the world from Communism, or of assuring that the Good Guys will win all their wars against the Bad Guys, or any of a thousand other objectives that men set for themselves. God cannot be "used" for our purposes at all. When we become Christians, we offer ourselves to be used for *Christ's* purposes. When we pray, it is not a matter of "Listen, Lord, for thy servant speaketh," but "Speak, Lord, for thy servant heareth." Christianity is an experience and process by which sinners are made into children of God. This life is warfare; tomorrow's life is rest. But one should quickly add that even in this life there is peace in the midst of warfare and rest in the midst of struggle.

I now propose, in the remainder of this chapter, to apply the insights we have gathered to the problems of our life in the here and now. Specifically, we shall raise the issue of what can be expected as the present "answer" to the problems of sin, achievement, suffering, and death, in the light of the truth that our perfect salvation is yet to come. In short, how much imperfection are we stuck with in this life?

Take sin. As Christians we are sinners saved by grace. How much are we saved? That question cannot be solved by use of a tape measure. But both facts remain true. This means that we cannot be perfectionistic, either about ourselves (which we are not likely to be anyway) or about others (which we *are* likely to be). We are not going to be perfect in this life—not in character, certainly, although some think we can perfectly love Christ. This is a dangerous thing to say. It needs explanation, lest Christians sit down in the middle of their sins and decide that sinning, being human, is inevitable. People who think this way ought to ask themselves just which sin it is that they must inevitably commit. They will, of course, find that there is none, absolutely none. What then do we mean when we say that we shall never be perfect until the age to come?

In brief, we can put it this way. We may have victory over all known sin. No Christian has to be in bondage to some habit he cannot break. But growth will always mean the recognition of heretofore unnoticed sins and the necessity of dealing with them. This means that the goal of Christlikeness is infinitely approachable but never reachable. No arbitrary limits can be placed beforehand on how near to Christ we can grow. At first this seems odd, but we are familiar with this kind of situation in other areas of human interest. For example, in mathematics. For those who can remember their high school geometry, the value of *pi* is just such a value—infinitely approachable but never reachable. But since some of us cannot remember back that far, we can illustrate this truth more simply. Try dividing 3 into 10. It goes 3 times; but not exactly, for one unit is left over. If the division is carried one step farther, it would be 3.3. If carried still farther, 3.33. And still farther, 3.333. And still farther, 3.3333. Now a person could spend the rest of his life adding threes after the decimal and he would be getting constantly nearer the true value of 10 divided by 3, but he could never finish off the process, as you can see for yourself, if you try it for five minutes. The absolute answer will elude him, because there can be no stopping place.

Our inability to become sinlessly perfect replicas of Jesus Christ in the here-and-now is sometimes attributed to the fact that we have two natures struggling within us. I think that is a mistaken way of putting it. Paul suggests in Colossians 3:9-10 that we have "put off" the old nature and "put on" the new nature. What struggles within us is not two natures but two orders—the old order and the New Order; or, to put it differently, today and Tomorrow. In our spirits we are part of the New Order. We have been born from above and have become partakers of the divine nature. The powers of the world to come have already taken up their abode within us. But while in spirit we belong to the New, in body we belong to the old. Our bodies have not yet been redeemed (Rom. 8:23). Meanwhile, the environment in which we function (except for the new environment provided by the fellowship of believers, and this is mixed) belongs to the old, so there are powerful temptations to sin in the structures of evil resident in society. We are called to live according to the standards and structures of Tomorrow, while life itself is carried on in today. This is our problem. It drives the believer to his knees in prayer, trust, and commitment to Christ, who is the Lord even of today.

To this problem, we have the answer in Christ, but not the solution except in promise (though still in Christ). That is to say, the solution is the coming in triumph and power of God's New Order. This supplies the perfect environment for which we long. At the same time, the body must be transformed into the kind of body which is perfectly adapted to the New Order. This is what Paul calls in 1 Corinthians 15:44 a spiritual body, by which he means no doubt a body which is the perfectly adapted vehicle for the abode and expression of the redeemed spirit of man. This is complete redemption. But since all who have trusted in their Lord throughout history must share in his triumph, even as they believed and lived by his promises, this also means resurrection, and more specifically, resurrection of the body. Salvation will then be complete. Total man will then be totally saved.

So much for individual sin. Let us now apply the same logic to social sin. Obviously these two problems are related. If men are not going to be individually perfect in this present life, they are not likely to be socially perfect either. What can we hope for in our efforts to bring the social order into greater conformity with the revealed will of God? This is the problem at which we want to look now, and a lot of recent and some not-so-recent history is bound up with the search for an answer.

In the beginning was the social gospel of late 19th century and early 20th century fame. The social gospelers had a genuine social concern, but a theology inadequate to carry it. They spoke of "bringing in the kingdom of God" (as though it were in man's power to bring it in!) and of "perfecting the social structures of history." They were wrong. What happened next is a tragedy from which we now are only beginning to emerge. Fundamentalism, in reaction against one extreme, swung way over to another extreme. Since the church could not bring in the Kingdom (as they rightly saw), the church should not have anything at all to do with the social order (they wrongly reasoned). Social action was hopeless. Nothing could be done by the church in history except to pluck a few brands from the burning and "sit tight" until the Lord should come and set things right. Inconsistently, however, the fundamentalists did permit a social concern to express itself in two areas: gambling and liquor.

The social gospel suggested that the church (with the aid of the Holy Spirit, of course) could do everything. The fundamentalists countered with the idea that the church could do nothing. The truth—as happens so often—is in between. The church cannot do everything, but it definitely can do something. It can make some situations better than they are. But it cannot make things perfect, for perfection is the mark of God's Coming Order.

The church can do something because it is the community of resurrection. Already through it the powers of the world to come are at large in history. The Holy Spirit, who is its life, has honored its witness and given it victories through the long centuries of its existence. The church has made a difference in society. It would be an insult to its Lord to say that it has not. It has been the light of the world and the salt of the earth, out of all proportion to its size. The world would be a lot different if the church had never existed.

But at the same time, the fact of sin both in the world

and in the church puts limits to what the church can achieve in influencing society. It remains a community of hope. Every achievement it effects in the social order is precarious. What it successfully mends today may unravel tomorrow. An Englishman, J. B. Bury, in 1913 wrote a book extolling the triumph of the right to freedom of speech in the West —a hard-won victory. Just a few short years afterwards, we saw this "triumph" reversed in the rise of dictatorships and of the totalitarian states of Germany and Russia. In those lands, even the freedom to keep one's mouth shut was denied. Citizens were expected to applaud or to boo on signal.

Nor is precariousness our only problem here. Fragmentariness is another. While one part of the social fabric is being mended, big holes may be opening in another part. The trick of keeping all parts equally mended at once eludes us.

Even this is not all. Each advance in goodness brings with it, like an inescapable shadow, new forms of evil. The mother who cannot wait until her helpless infant is able to feed and clothe himself presently shudders to discover that her child, emancipated from helplessness, is now able to get into all sorts of new troubles.[3]

No, the church cannot change society into the kingdom of God on earth, but it can always do more than it does to change things for the better. Indeed, as the community of resurrection, it *must* try. For as such, in its own life, it represents Tomorrow. It is a "colony of Heaven," to use Moffatt's vivid translation of Philippians 3:20; it is the community of Tomorrow. As such, it must speak and live as though Tomorrow were already here, whatever the unbelieving world may say or do. It must assert the claims of

[3] Augustine once said that the fabled goodness of a little babe was due less to its pure heart than to its weak legs.

God's New Order, and in the light of it bring every social institution to judgment. It must never be satisfied with any status quo, but must demand without ceasing that the world take that New Order into account in all its reckonings. I say, "as though Tomorrow were already here." In one sense, Tomorrow *is* already here. It is here in a partial, fragmentary, imperfect way in the existence of the church as the community of resurrection. But it is also a community of hope, because it looks for that "city which hath foundations, whose builder and maker is God," the City whose coming means the end of things-as-they-are. That City is no human achievement. "It is your Father's good pleasure," promised our Lord, "to *give* you the kingdom" (Luke 12:32). The church lives in the here and now in the light of the Then and There.

We have looked at individual sin and social sin in order to interpret their persistence in the light of the truths established earlier in this chapter. Let us now look at another problem—the problem of suffering. To most people, this is the most perplexing problem of all. They can live with their sins, but they cannot endure suffering or stand to see their loved ones suffer. The fact of suffering presents a much more irritating problem than the fact of sin!

The problem is usually posed in the familiar question, "Why?" Men say, "If God is an all-loving God, and if he has the 'whole world in his hands,' why did this have to happen to me?" The logic lying behind such a question is not difficult to spot. It runs something like this: Premise one: A loving God would not let a good-living person suffer. (The phrase "good living" is usually, though not exclusively, a synonym for "decent" or "moral," and refers to some one who pays his debts, stays out of trouble, and goes to church.) Premise two: I am a good-living person. Inevitable conclusion: God will not let me suffer. No wonder such a person gets mixed up in his thinking when he considers the obvious fact that the world does not work that way!

And it doesn't! The Cross is proof of it. The greatest sufferer of all was the best-living man of all. Here is a puzzle. But it is a puzzle upon which God has shed much light, so if we hope to make any sense out of the fact of suffering, we had better take our clues from God. When we stand at the Cross, and look from that vantage point, certain interesting truths emerge. The first is: This is, indeed, God's world, but something has happened to it; it has gone off its moral and spiritual rocker. This means that a lot of horrible things happen in it that are highly displeasing to God, things that God does not cause—such as murders. A second truth is this: God has not deserted his lost and suffering world, but is in this thing up to his neck. He suffers with us and for us, and—most humbling of all—at our hands. A third truth is this: Through a love which suffers, God is exposing the exceeding sinfulness of sin (the ultimate cause of the world's suffering), judging it, and removing it. A fourth and final truth is this: God's omnipotence reveals itself in his ability to turn to his own good purposes the most evil intentions and the most wicked deeds of men. Men meant the Cross for evil; God used it for good. The greatest crime in history has become the source of man's greatest blessing. This is a sample of what God can do with all of history's blunders and sins.

It is important for our Christian understanding and living that we lay hold of these four truths. Two of them especially we need to pinpoint, if we want to say—as we certainly do—that the gospel has good news for sufferers. The first element in the good news is that God is in a long-term program to rid his universe of all suffering. True, this is the day of struggle and not of triumph. Only in God's New

Order will the triumph be complete. Nonetheless, the triumph is sure and we can rejoice in its promise. Meanwhile, Tomorrow shines beforehand into our hearts today, giving us peace in and victory over our own sufferings, even as we offer them to Christ for use in his cause. By now we recognize the familiar pattern we have already noted in other connections in this chapter. The powers of the world to come are already here at our disposal and for our peace, even while we wait for that New Order in which faith will be swallowed up in sight and suffering will be no more.

But we wait. Meanwhile suffering continues to be a fact and Christians are caught up in it. What then? Why then we must adjust our attitude toward it so that the purposes of God may be fulfilled through our suffering. What makes suffering so unbearable is not suffering in itself, but its meaninglessness, its pointlessness. It seems like such a senseless, wasteful thing. It is to this feeling that the Christian faith addresses itself by telling us that if we offer our suffering to Christ for his use, our pain can acquire meaning. As Christians we do not *resign* ourselves to suffering, nor stoically *steel* ourselves to it, nor patiently *submit* to it as the inscrutable will of God. Instead, we *use* it, use it to advance the cause of our Lord Jesus Christ, to whom we have yielded everything, including our suffering.

For what can suffering be used? For two things: one, our Christian growth and perfection; the other, the good of others.

There is at the close of the Sermon on the Mount a hint as to the relation between our growth and adversity. It is in the story of the house that was built on a rock and the house that was built on the sand (Matt. 7:24-27). Both houses got the same bad weather, but one stood and the other fell. This is a parable of life. There are rock-built lives and sand-built lives, lives rightly related to God and lives wrongly related to God. The difference is not at all in the weather they get in life. Sometimes good people get more bad weather than wicked people. The difference is in what happens when the winds blow and the floods rise. That difference is this: The lives built on sand become embittered and poisoned by suffering, but the lives built on rock do not. Why not? Our Lord does not come right out and say it in this passage, but the author of Hebrews does when he says that even Christ was perfected through sufferings (Heb. 2:10). Even as Christ was fitted to be the captain of our salvation through the things that he suffered, so we can take every brickbat that life throws our way and make it a building block in the life-edifice that the Holy Spirit is constructing. The Holy Spirit is able to do this, if we offer up our sufferings to him in love. Furthermore, there is a special outflow of the love of Christ, special experiences of intimacy and understanding with him, when this is done. Only sufferers can know certain aspects of the suffering love of Christ. They hold a special place in God's heart.

Not only can our sufferings be used as instruments to enrich our own lives, but also they can be used to serve others, and thus advance the cause of Christ. This is the point of Thornton Wilder's play called, "The Angel that Troubled the Waters." The play is based on the biblical story of the pool of Bethesda, where the first to step into the pool after its waters had been troubled by an angel was healed (John 5:2-4). A physician with a wound he cannot heal stands by the pool, patiently waiting for the troubling of the waters. As he stands there, an angel addresses him, stating that the healing to be had at that pool is not for him. Without his wound, so the angel explains, he would lose all his powers as a physician. He would be unable to heal others. It was precisely because he himself had suffered that he could being comfort and healing to others. In Love's service, so he was told, only the wounded soldiers can serve.

This is true of those sufferings for which the use-value can be seen. It is equally true of those whose use-value cannot be seen. Leonard Hodgson is surely right when he says that wherever pain is borne in such a way that it is prevented from breeding bitterness or any evil fruit, a contribution has been made to the rescuing of God's creation from Satan's grip. But I think we can be even more positive in our approach to suffering than this. I think we can say that wherever suffering is endured in the spirit of loving acceptance, there we are involved in filling up that which is lacking in the sufferings of Christ (Col. 1:24). Human beings are all interconnected, and Christians, like their suffering Savior, can suffer vicariously for the needs of others. We can serve our Lord not only in deeds of mercy but also in suffering, for suffering is itself an action, a way of working for his Kingdom. This is the meaning of the Cross. In ways beyond our knowing, our sufferings, like our lives themselves, are caught up in the ongoing sweep of God's kingdom and used for God's glory. We minister through our pain, as Christ in his greater way did through his. We then become broken bread and poured out wine for the sins of the world.

People who think that only bad people should suffer and that all good people should be exempt, surely have never given the matter much thought. How self-righteous we would become, how unsympathetic, how hard! After all, why in that case *should* we be sympathetic? The sufferer is only suffering his just deserts. If he were good, like us, he would not have to go through all that pain. Similarly, what a gap would grow between the world and the Christian. The Christian could not go to the cancer-stricken, or to those whose sons have been killed in battle, or to those whose child has been run over by a truck and speak of the comforting mercies of Christ. He could not say, "I have been right where you are, and I know what Christ can mean in such a situation." If the Christian were exempt from suffering, he could not say anything helpful to people in trouble because he had never been there himself. The constantly sunny weather in which he lived would divide him from those unfortunates who were the victims of life's storms.

No, God's way is better. Dorothy Sayers reminds us that God does not abolish our sufferings, but transforms them. He did not stop the crucifixion, but rather raised Christ from the dead. The Christian can even be *grateful* in suffering, for he knows that "all things work together for good to them that love God" (Rom. 8:28). The man whose attitudes are right is delivered from evil; all things, even the mistakes and hates of others, have been turned to his good, by the power of God. Or, as Grubb has put it, "Good and evil are not in our circumstances, but in ourselves, according to our reaction to them."[4]

But Tomorrow is another story. The gospel assures us that when God's kingdom comes in its fullness, all sorrow and suffering will be eliminated from God's universe and we shall live happily eternally. That is good news indeed!

Let me summarize briefly what we have done, before we turn to one final illustration of how the church both possesses and does not possess redemption, how it is at one and the same time the community of resurrection-life and the community of hope. I have tried to show how power over sin is secured for the believer through Christ's victory over sin, although the tantalizing, tempting presence of sin continues until the final triumph of the kingdom of God. Only at that time will its presence be removed. Similarly, power

[4] Norman Grubb, *op. cit.*, p. 89.

over suffering is secured to the believer by participation in Christ's victory over suffering (1 Pet. 2:21-23); but the presence of suffering, with all its temptation to resentment and bitterness remains until the final triumph of God's kingdom. Only at that point will its presence be removed. In both of these cases, the Christian can fall flat on his face in humiliating impotence and failure if he does not obey the injunction of the conquering Christ who said, "Follow (i.e., stay close to) me." Now, in addition to sin and suffering, there is a third enemy of man for which this same situation is true; namely, death.

Christ triumphed over death. We share his triumph, yet the presence of death remains, just as though nothing had happened. We still die! What then does it mean to share his triumph, to be the community of resurrection here and now? (The term "community of resurrection" here begins to take on fresh meaning.) It means, for one thing, that the fear of death is removed. We who have seen the Future in Jesus Christ and into whose lives the Future has come through the shedding abroad of the Holy Spirit in our hearts, know that we have a future, even beyond death. We know that nothing, neither life nor death, can separate us now from the love of God, which is in Christ Jesus our Lord (Rom. 8:38-39). This means that we no longer fear that death means either annihilation or condemnation. But there is more to it even than that. It means that death's triumph over us is temporary and provisional. Just as Christ rose from the dead and has given to us his resurrection life, so we too shall rise from the dead, sharing in the final triumph of God's New Order in and through a glorified, resurrection body of our own. For a man is not a spirit imprisoned in a body. If he were, he could be a complete person as spirit. But a man is rather a spirit and a body in combination, and he cannot be a complete person without a body, which is the means for identification and for communication. The Christian word, then, is not "immortality," but rather "resurrection." In the day of resurrection, death, along with sorrow, suffering, and sin will be swept into the discard and only God will count (Rev. 21:4).

Our look at the gospel is now finished. As we saw in our opening chapter, the gospel, from start to finish, is the story of Jesus Christ—of what he did back there in his then-body, of what he does in the Christian era through his now-body, and of what he will do tomorrow in his coming in glory. It is his story, all the way. As Kierkegaard suggests, the Christian era itself is but a parenthesis in the life of Christ. The Christ who *was* is the very same Christ who *will be.*

Then where are we today? Who knows? We do not know whether we are in the fourth act of history's great drama or the tenth. Indeed, we do not know how many acts there will be. We do know that like every mystery story, the windup will untangle all the threads that have puzzled us and everything that has happened will fall into place in one great understandable plot. We also know that everybody who has played in the drama will be brought back on the stage for the Grand Finale, some to great applause and some to terrible condemnation and judgment. We know one other thing. The wisdom and the majesty and the power of the Author of man's salvation will be the source of never-ending amazement to those whose eyes are then fully opened.

But we must give Bishop Berggrav, of Norway, the last word. He says it best. The figure of speech is different, but the truth is the same. Speaking at the Christian Youth

Conference at Oslo a few years ago, the Bishop pointed upward to the ceiling of the Cathedral and said:

> "Did you observe the ceiling of this church? It is low and heavy. The atmosphere is made oppressive. Why is it like this? Surely, there is no such intention in it, but as a matter of fact, it becomes today a symbol of the whole situation of men. I wish I could take away this temporary ceiling, now eleven years since it was put in. Then you would see the most lovely and mighty scenery, prepared through these eleven years by one of our Norwegian painters. He needed this temporary low ceiling as the floor of his workroom. In one year we hope to have the view of what is above. Then you will have the most convincing sermon which painting can give of Christ the Lord. But you could not see it today, just as it is not given to us today to see Christ as the actual Lord of the world. But He is! When the low ceiling of life in time is taken away, you will get to know that He was there all the time, and that the low ceiling of today was His working floor."[5]

D. T. Niles (to whom we are indebted for this illustration) adds, "He will come, the ceiling of this life will be lifted, and then we shall see what our great God has accomplished." Surely we can add with the biblical writer, "Even so, come, Lord Jesus."

[5] From *That They May Have Life,* by Daniel T. Niles. (New York: Harper & Brothers, Copyright, 1951). Used by permission.

5

THE DIVINE GOSPEL AND THE HUMAN RESPONSE

THE GOSPEL OF GOD—words cannot tell the wonder of it! But the church of God—words can tell all too well the weakness of it! Christ is wonderful, but the community which bears his name is something else again. In speaking of the church, I am not referring to some invisible entity that exists in the mind of God. I am referring to the actual, visible, concrete group which bears the name "Christian" in the world today. I am referring to all the denominations which, in their organized life, bear responsibility before the world for the reputation of the Christian cause. "Oh, but all these groups are not to be equated with the community of faith, hope, and love of which the New Testament speaks. The churches of today have in them many unbelievers who have never tasted of the powers of the world to come. The true church is a kind of church-within-a-church; that is to say, the true church is the genuinely redeemed group within the mixed multitudes that make up organized Christianity." There is truth in that contention, but it merely points up the pathetic nature of our modern situation. How did all these people who have no real faith in or love for Jesus Christ get into our churches?

It would be nice to be able to answer that question by saying, "infant baptism." Certainly, the habit of baptizing infants has not helped any. Indeed, infant baptism has been called a scandal by some of the very people who practice it.

But there is one big obstacle in the way of putting the blame on the practice of infant baptism. It is this: Those who bar infant baptism and pride themselves on insisting upon a conversion experience prior to baptism do not appear to build any better churches than their brethren. When Dean Inge said that the church was a secular institution where the half-educated cater for the half-converted, he was talking of your church along with the rest.

The "half-converted"! It is a disturbing term. But it surely puts the finger on the place which hurts the most. There has been something wrong with the process by which we make Christians. Our evangelism has been defective. After all has been said about the weakness of human nature, after all the talk about the tendency of many to begin bravely only to grow cold later, and after all the discussion about people falling away through nobody's fault but their own, still it is the conversion process itself that needs re-examination. Christianity is not a culture-religion, like so many other modern religions. One does not become a Christian by being born into a certain kind of civilization—like that of modern America. Strait is the gate and narrow is the way to life, and each must seek and find it for himself. Becoming a Christian is a matter of personal decision. "Except ye be converted . . . ye shall not enter into the kingdom of heaven" (Matt. 18:3).

Now, the trouble is that there are fake forms of conversion, fake forms which can be easily substituted for the real thing. Unless we understand the fake forms, we shall never understand the true form. To them, then, let us turn first.

Fake form number one is a doctrinal conversion.[1] A doctrinal conversion is a conversion from one set of ideas to

[1] The terms I am using, "doctrinal conversion" and, later, "emotional conversion," were first suggested to me by my former colleague, Dr. W. E. Powers.

another set of ideas. Here, for instance, is an atheist. He does not believe in God, Christ, immortality, or any such thing. Presently he becomes firmly convinced of the truth of these and other doctrines of the Christian faith. Is he then a Christian? By no means—not if that is all that you can say for him. He has merely exchanged one set of ideas for another. (The same could be said, of course, for a convert from another religion.) His trouble is that he is merely a spectator of the drama whose truth he affirms. He believes that Christ is the Savior of the world, that he died for man's sins, that in his resurrection he overcame all of life's enemies; but he believes these things as one who sits in the grandstand and watches the game being played. He himself is not personally involved. These are mere truths to be believed. His conversion is intellectual only. It is as though a friend came to me in my desperate illness and told me all he knew about a certain doctor whose skill could cure me—his age, his address, his telephone number, his educational background, and the size of his family. Then, having elicited from me the assurance that I do indeed believe all that he has told me concerning the doctor, wrings my hand enthusiastically and congratulates me on my healing!

We must always remember that no set of ideas has saving power. What we seek is not the power of theological ideas, but the power of the living God. It is not good views that we need, but good news—news in which we can share by personal appropriation. As Robert MacAfee Brown has reminded us: God was not in a statement; God was in Christ. Joseph Fort Newton was equally trenchant when he said that a man can believe in the resurrection of the body and still be dead in soul.

Doctrines are important, but never as ends in themselves. Rather, they are means to an end. They are like signposts; they point beyond themselves. A sign giving the direction and distance of a certain city can be very helpful. But woe to the man who sits on the signpost itself, as though that were the solution of his travel problem. Woe, too, to a man who latches on to doctrines as though they could take him where he wants to go. They cannot do so. They can only point him beyond themselves to the Lamb of God who takes away the sin of the world. A doctrinal conversion, a conversion to a set of ideas, is not a Christian conversion.

Neither is a merely emotional conversion a Christian conversion. Those of us who are members of denominations who emphasize (and rightly) the value of experience are especially vulnerable at this point. Let us therefore make clear what we mean by an emotional conversion. Let us take the actual case of Edith Moule. When she was a child she was in an evangelistic meeting where they sang a hymn which was sad and deeply moving ("There Is a Fountain Filled with Blood"). Gripped by the song, she started to cry. Her minister approach her and asked if she believed that Jesus Christ died for her sins [a purely doctrinal question, note, which he did not follow up with anything further]. She answered, "Yes." She had been reared in a Christian home and had always believed this. Then the minister put his hand on her shoulder and led in prayer, thanking God that she had come under conviction of sin. "That," said Edith Moule years later, "was where he made his mistake. I had had no conviction of sin at all. I was crying because the music was sad and the emotion of the moment had gotten me." But the minister told her that she was converted, and because he said so she tried to believe it. She told her family and relatives, and they in their happiness bought her a Bible and a prayer book and she tried to be good. So another unredeemed person was added to the rolls of the church.

I am sure this story sounds very familiar to many of my

readers. It is an oft-repeated pattern—so much so that Billy Graham some years ago said that he had stopped ending his sermons with tear-evoking stories, because he found so many people coming down the aisle crying over the story instead of over their sins.

An emotional conversion may be defined as a conversion to a feeling. Its end is sentimentality. The emotionally converted man spends the major portion of his Christian life trying to feel right. If he feels right, he is sure that all is well between him and God. But if for any reasons the feeling is not there, he runs to find it again. He goes to church, to evangelistic services, and to Bible conferences in order to have the feeling. If a particular minister cannot produce it, the man obviously is not spiritual. If a church cannot nourish it, the church is cold and formal and unspiritual. The feeling is everything. Rarely indeed is such a person noted for his ethics or his concern for Christian living. Impulses toward the latter are diverted by the sentimentality inherent in that type of conversion.

There is an element of truth in all this that needs to be preserved, even as there is in the concern for doctrine. But in spite of this fact, the emotional conversion must be sternly rejected as spurious. Why? Because a feeling does not in and of itself indicate anything—least of all, redemption. There may be many reasons why the emotion exists. It may be merely mob psychology and the whole experience a merely human response to the mood of the moment. There may be more than this. The experience may be accompanied by a genuine sense of relief, such as happens when a person talks to someone else about a problem and finishes the monologue by saying, "I feel much better already." Here nothing has really happened beyond the psychological sense of having got something off one's chest.

But there may be more to an emotional conversion than

this. There even may be an actual experience of God, but not a redemptive experience. It is possible to feel the presence of God, but not experience his life-changing power. I am convinced that many people who can refer in all sincerity to an experience that they once had of God and who therefore think they have been converted fall in this category. I would say that they experienced the reality of God but not his saving grace. The proof that it is one rather than the other is found in the fact that there is no carry-over. Life goes on as it was; there is no reorientation. This shows that the merely emotional conversion is not a Christian conversion.

There is a third kind of fake conversion: a moral conversion. This is a conversion to a set of ideals. A person who has been morally bad becomes morally good. In place of one set of conduct patterns, he acquires another which is more acceptable and praiseworthy. But conversion to a set of ideals is not a Christian conversion.

I hope that I am making myself clear. I am not attacking either doctrine, emotion, or morals. I am for all three. But I am saying as emphatically as I can that a conversion to a system of ideas, or to a kind of feeling, or to a set of ideals is not a Christian conversion—not even if you put all three of them together. I am adding, furthermore, that unless our churches learn to distinguish between the true and the false, and learn to guard against the false, our evangelism is going to be sadly compromised. The fact of the matter is, a person can be converted to almost anything—to the minister, to the church, to the youth program, to the church school—and none of these, either singly or together with others, adds up to a Christian conversion.

The trouble with a doctrinal or emotional or moral conversion is the same in each case. No one of them is able to get me outside of myself. In each case I am left, in the loneliness of my own selfhood, with a set of ideas, or with a good feeling, or with a set of ideals. None of these things can save. As a person, my deepest need is for another person. This is true even on the level of my normal human experience. He that is rich in ideas and ideals, but who loves no one and has no one to love. him is poor indeed. A person needs persons. But we must say more. A person—finite, creaturely, anxious—needs The Person. A Christian is one who has a passion for The Person, and that Person is Jesus Christ. It is in Jesus Christ that God has given himself to be known. A Christian conversion is conversion to Jesus Christ. It is the establishment of right relations with a living Lord and Savior.

We now are back where we began in our very first chapter. The message of evangelism is Jesus Christ, the Savior and Lord—Jesus Christ who wrought so mightily on Calvary's tree, Jesus Christ who is present so powerfully today, Jesus Christ who will work so mightily and triumphantly tomorrow. We present to people not only a "plan of salvation," but also Him. When we seek for decisions, what we ask for is not merely a belief in the Sacrifice, but trusting obedience to the sovereign Lord for life and death and everything in between.

It is not possible to separate Christ's Lordship from his Saviorhood. To hear some people tell it, you can have Christ as your Savior, but the Devil for your Lord. This cannot be. There can be no saving grace emanating from Jesus Christ except in and through an acknowledgment of his Lordship. To believe in a redemptive way means to acquire a Lord. It means to invite the skill of Another to be brought to bear upon your need. When this happens there are doctrinal ideas involved; when this happens there often are deep emotional overtones (especially when we realize that we have been pardoned and accepted); when this happens morality follows. But the establishment of interpersonal relations with Jesus Christ is none of these, but something quite different. It is redemption in holy love.

The formula for finding Christ is repentance and faith. But unfortunately, these words too have become twisted from their basic meaning and hence need to be reminted. Take repentance. It does not mean being sorry for our sins. It may be that when we repent we *are* sorry for our sins. But that is not the heart of the matter. In fact, sorrow for sins can be a block to our spiritual growth, for remorse fixes our attention on what we are trying to avoid. When our minds are centered on what we are trying to avoid, they tend to thrust us into the very acts which we fear to commit. This follows from a well-known psychological law—the law of reversed effort. It can be illustrated quite simply. Suppose you put on the ground a foot-wide plank and try to walk the length of it. It probably will not be at all difficult. But suppose this same plank is lifted fifty feet in the air, with nothing between you and the ground. Suppose you now start to walk the length of it. You probably will never make it. You will be so fearful of falling, so determined not to fall, so filled with horror at the thought of falling, that you will fall. The very effort to avoid falling will plunge you headlong into space. The same thing is true with respect to sin. If your sin haunts you, if you are remorseful day and night, if you are determined not to slip again, if the very thought of such a thing fills you with horror, get ready to fall! God is not trying to make us feel remorse for sin, but to lift us out of sin. Repentance is not a backward look of remorse, but a forward look of reorientation.

Repentance means to adopt God's way of looking at things: God's way of seeing yourself, God's way of seeing the solution of your sin-problem, God's way of seeing life and its responsibilities, God's way of looking at the world. To repent is to renounce the past and to turn your back on what you were, what you did, and on how you viewed things. To repent is to be caught up already into redemption.

Then how about that other word, faith? We already have seen that faith is not believing that such-and-such a thing is true. That would be to make Christianity a set of ideas, to be tossed about from mind to mind like cash is tossed from pocket to pocket. But having said this I must immediately add the other side of this truth. Faith cannot arise without doctrinal ideas. It is a strange notion indeed —and the fact that many people who ought to know better have adopted it, does not lessen its strangeness—that tells us that we can commit ourselves in trustful obedience to a person about whom we have no information. Surely it is clear that such an idea is an absurdity. It is also clear how the idea arose. It arose in the effort to break sharply with the theory that to have faith is to believe a set of ideas. But fortunately we do not have to land in one untruth in order to avoid another untruth. Genuine faith involves the whole man, including his mind, and while mental assent is not faith, faith cannot exist without mental assent.

The object of faith is Jesus Christ. What is the minimum amount of information about him that we need to have in order to make him the object of our faith? Far be it from me to say what has to be known and what can be omitted, for faith to operate. Let me say, rather, that what is usually presented for mental acceptance to the unbeliever is that Christ is the Son of God and that he died for our sins. If the speaker is pressed to explain further what is meant by saying that Christ died for our sins, he may very well add that it means that Christ took our place, that at the cross he bore the penalty of our sins, that his death was a substitutionary one.

Christ our substitute. What does *that* mean? When we raise this question we are putting ourselves once more in a position to understand why our evangelistic efforts have gone astray in filling our churches with people instead of filling people with God.

The word "substitute" can point in two opposite directions, according to whether my substitute absolves me from something or commits me to something. Illustrations will make my meaning clear. In the Civil War, I am told, it was possible for a man of wealth to hire someone to serve in the army for him. His substitute did the fighting for him; he himself thereby was absolved from serving. Similarly, if an anonymous donor pays my hospital bill, I do not have to pay it; I am absolved. Once more, if Dr. X cannot make his scheduled address but sends a substitute, then obviously the obligation of Dr. X has been met. He does not have to make an address.

But there is another use of the word "substitute" which points in exactly the opposite direction. The relation of our ambassadors to our Secretary of State in the national government illustrate this latter form of substitution. The Secretary of State cannot be in every country at once to represent the American government. So he sends ambassadors to live in the different countries of the world in his stead, to substitute for him as representatives of the State Department. But here the Secretary of State is not absolved by his substitutes from doing anything; on the contrary, he is committed. When the ambassador threatens in the name of the United States Government, the Secretary of State is committed to backing him up. When the ambassador makes a promise in the name of the United States Government, the Secretary is committed to making good on the promise. So long as the ambassador is not repudiated and recalled home, what he says and does commits the Secretary of State.

It is of the utmost importance, therefore, that we know which kind of substitution we are talking about when we say that Christ died for us. If we think that his death settled it all so that we are absolved from every claim that God has upon us, we become the victims of what Dietrich Bonhoeffer called "cheap grace." "Cheap grace," writes Bonhoeffer, "is the deadly enemy of the church."[2] It operates on the basis that since the account has been paid in advance, everything can be had for nothing. In such a church "the world finds a covering for its sins; no contrition is required, still less any real desire to be delivered from sin." Bonhoeffer goes on to point out that cheap grace is the justification of sin without the justification of the sinner. Grace alone does everything, it is said, and so everything can remain as it was before. "Cheap grace is the preaching of forgiveness without requiring repentance, baptism without church discipline, communion without confession, absolution without contrition. Cheap grace is grace without discipleship, grace without the Cross, grace without Jesus Christ, living and incarnate." Instead of opening up the way to Christ, cheap grace has closed it; it has hardened us in our disobedience. "The word of cheap grace has been the ruin of more Christians than any command of works."

Strong words; deserved words; words that go to the heart of much of the sickness of our American Christianity. What, then, is the alternative to cheap grace? The alternative is costly grace, grace which means discipleship. Note that costly grace is still grace. Salvation is all of God and of his mercy; not one iota of it is of man or of man's merit. But it is costly, both because it cost Jesus Christ his life's blood to make it effective, and further because it costs us a com-

[2] From *The Cost of Discipleship*, by Dietrich Bonhoeffer (New York: The Macmillan Company, Copyright, 1953). Scattered quotations from pages 37-48. Used by permission.

plete giving up of ourselves. "I would give everything that I have," said the young Christian, "to have a Christian experience and testimony like yours." "That's exactly what it cost me," said the veteran; "everything I had."

Costly grace—which is grace in the New Testament sense—is connected with our second usage of the word "substitute." We are not absolved by the death of Christ from all the claims of God upon us; we are not now set free to go our own way because the debt has been paid. We are indeed set free and forgiven, but in such a way that we become committed to something. As our substitute in the sense of our representative, Christ commits us by his death and resurrection to—death and resurrection!

We are now—and only now, as far as this chapter is concerned—in a position to define what it means to have faith. Faith is identification, identification with Jesus Christ. In order to identify with him, I have to know something about him; but the knowledge about him is not faith, for the knowledge about him can be held in the mind and assented to without the movement of faith. Faith, I repeat, is identification. It has two aspects, a negative and a positive. The negative aspect is the realization of my own nothingness and helplessness. "Nothing in my hand I bring; simply to thy cross I cling." Nothingness is another word for complete dependence. It is the mark of our creaturehood, both as created and as redeemed. To say that we are creatures is to say that at every moment we are dependent on something (Someone) not ourselves. We are receivers, not originators. But sin means that we have forgotten this fact. In our pride, we have decided that we can run our own lives; so we set out to establish our own lives, in our own strength, according to our own blueprint. Redemption can only take place when this whole enterprise is repudiated and abandoned and the structures of selfhood that have been built on this foundation have been shattered. But we cannot will our own death in this way; the self that we have so carefully put together is the only self we know. The shattering of this self, death to this self, is only possible in and through Jesus Christ. When we identify with him, we thereby are acknowledging our own helplessness. We cannot save ourselves; he and he alone is the Savior. We are completely dependent on his skill. This is the negative aspect of our identification.

The positive aspect is the understanding that he commits us to all that he is as the perfect image of God; i.e., to true humanity. We become committed to following him in discipleship, to living his life, to holding his objectives, to being interested in his interests, to praying his kind of prayers, to loving with his kind of love. But only "in Christ." We are not renewed by him in order to be turned loose to operate as Christians on our own initiative. To identify with Christ is to acknowledge that only in union with him is any of this possible. We are drawn up and incorporated into him.

Faith as identification is written on every page of the New Testament. First, Christ identified with us. Though he was rich, for our sakes he became poor. He sat where we sit. He stood where we stand. He took upon himself our weakness, our sin, our sorrow, our destiny. He entered into all our liabilities that we might enter into all his assets. And we do this by identifying with him. He did not die in order to absolve us from death, but in order to commit us to death—death to self and to sin. We are crucified with Christ. Similarly we are risen with Christ. Similarly we are victorious with Christ. We reign with Christ. We share in his mighty work of redemption. What he was and did, we become and do. To believe is to identify and to identify is to commit oneself to Another, to become receptive and open to a life not our own. It is to become united with Christ.

Christ was and is Representative Man. He lived a representative life. He died a representative death. He rose in a representative resurrection. He is now glorified in a representative glorification. There is a Man in the heavenlies —the head of a new race.

The link between that Man and the believer is the Holy Spirit. But since the word "link" sounds like something external, let us say rather that we are united with Christ and incorporated into his life by the Holy Spirit. The Holy Spirit is not something separate from Christ. He is Christ—in Spirit. As Paul says, "The Lord is that Spirit" (2 Cor. 3:17). Yet we must not simply identify the Holy Spirit with Christ. This would make us have only two members of the Trinity instead of three. It is the function of the Holy Spirit to make the Jesus Christ of history, the now reigning Lord, immediately present to our hearts. To know the Holy Spirit is to know Christ and is also to know God. However, we must not separate the members of the Trinity so that we get three Gods. But let us bypass this discussion, lest it lead us astray from the practical concern with the gospel which is our real task. Let us merely say that it is the Holy Spirit who makes Jesus Christ present and available to us.

By the Holy Spirit, Jesus Christ becomes my contemporary and I become his contemporary. I see myself at the foot of his cross and acknowledge that the sins of Judas, Caiaphas, Herod, Pilate, and the mob are my sins too. I crucified Jesus, and I tell him so in asking for pardon. He personally stands before me through the Holy Spirit. It is the Crucified One with whom I am dealing when I bend the knee in contrition. But now the Crucified One to whom I have addressed myself—acknowledging my oneness in sin with those who nailed him to the tree—addresses me in return, and says, "I was there too. But I died for those who crucified me and so I died for you." At this moment of personal confrontation, what was general becomes particular and for me personally. He died for all men in general. But when I address him in confession and need, he looks at me and says, "Yes, if you had been the only person in the world whose sin needed atonement when I hung upon the tree, I would have endured it all for your sake." In that moment I become his and he becomes mine. Calvary and Easter become a present experience in my life. The historical Christ becomes the internal Christ. By his Holy Spirit he becomes the guest of my soul with the intent of living his life all over again in me. This is redemption, as we have seen. All of this is opened up and made possible by a *Christian* conversion.

It is far, far better for the health of the Christian movement to have a disciplined, committed minority calling itself by the name of Christ than to fill our churches with an undisciplined, uninterested, unmoved rabble. The Communists should have taught us this. They always are more interested in quality than in quantity. It costs something to be a member of the Communist party. A Communist is indoctrinated, tested, disciplined, commanded. It costs nothing to be a member of the Christian church, nothing but an upraised hand and a monosyllabic grunt when the pastor raises the question of intent. We have auctioned off the gospel to the lowest bidder. We have made it seem a cheap and cut-rate thing. It must always be remembered that the fact that it is freely offered does not mean that it is cheap.

The implication of all this is that the churches themselves are an excellent field for evangelization. This is true in both the obvious sense and in a less obvious sense. In the obvious sense, which stems from what was stated in the last paragraph, the churches need to be evangelized because in them are members who have never had a head-on collision with Jesus Christ. But there is a deeper sense in which the churches need to be evangelized. Why? Because in the lives of their members there are unevangelized areas. Some blockage has occurred, some places exist in their lives where the Lordship of Christ is not acknowledged, some places where what was once surrendered to him in principle is kept back when the actual cost of surrender is spelled out in detail. For one reason or another, their commitment is incomplete. To evangelize here is to preach the gospel in such a way that the Word of God may be heard in some part of the life heretofore unyielded to Christ's will. If heard and responded to so that the sovereign rights of Jesus Christ are then acknowledged where they were not acknowledged before, then a person who is already a Christian (let us assume) has become evangelized at a deeper level.

I am not confusing Christian education and evangelism. It seems to me that Christian education cannot in and of itself go beyond the degree of commitment which the Christian permits. Education draws out what is implicit in my stand. But if I am inwardly dodging the will of Christ in my business life, for example, while trying to retain it in my home life and church life, no amount of education as to how a Christian should act in business will avail. As we can see with the race problem, you can always rationalize away the truth and find excuses for not acting according to it. What is needed is not more information, but a deeper surrender and commitment to Christ. When the gospel is so preached to a defeated, immature Christian that a decision is made and a hitherto jealously guarded area of life is surrendered to Christ, this too is evangelism. The evangel has again done its judging and renewing work.

I could not close this chapter without a word of a different type. It is possible so to warn the Christian worker about the pitfalls that await him, so to urge upon him the necessity of proper preparation, so to stress his need of knowing the meaning and the content of the gospel, that he despairs of ever being adequate to speak to another about Jesus Christ, and decides to leave it all to the professionals. If this were the final impact of this book, then nothing could be sadder or more tragic. It is the layman who has been my reader, not the minister. It is to help him become a more effective minister of Jesus Christ (yes, I know what I am saying; every layman is a minister) that this book has been written. Not one word do I retract about the great need and value of an informed laity. But information is not our greatest need, not even theological information. Theological professors as a class are not noted for their great evangelistic passion. Information must be wedded to motivation, and the latter is even more important than the former.

If we want to raise the question, "Who is sufficient for these things?" the only answer is, "No one." Certainly not the theologian or the pastor, and certainly not the layman. The thought of putting unholy or ignorant hands upon the souls of men must give us all pause. If surgery is a matter of life and death, how much more is evangelism? Let us be comforted, however, by the fact that, in the last analysis, we are not called to be evangelists. There is only one Evangelist, Jesus Christ, the risen Lord himself. We are called to a less terrifying vocation, the vocation of a witness. We witness to those things which we most surely know, and somehow our faltering, stumbling, limited efforts are caught up into Christ's on-going purposes and are used for the blessing of men. Men are never more blessed, and witnessing is never more effective, than when a heart that is aflame with the love of Christ is laid flush upon the anxious, darkened heart of a lost man or woman.

A full heart is infinitely better than a filled mind. But why make it an either-or? Why must we choose between the hot but ignorant heart and the cold but informed mind? We have been bidden to love the Lord our God with everything we are and have—with all our heart, with all our soul, with all our strength, with all our mind (Luke 10:27). All our faculties are to be at God's disposal, including the mind. If a full heart is better than a filled mind, then a full heart aided and guided by an informed mind is best of all. We each offer for God's use all of what we have, and we find to our glad surprise that when it is linked to his infinity, it is enough.

Appendix A

THE FATE OF THE HEATHEN WHO HAVE
NEVER HEARD

THE PROBLEM OF THE FATE of the heathen who have never heard the gospel appears to be of perennial interest to many people. The answer can only be conjectural, for there is no clear statement about it in the Scriptures. One must piece together as best one can such scraps of information as may seem to point to a solution. What follows is my effort at such "piecing." Others will "solve" the problem differently.

We must begin with the finality of Jesus Christ and take seriously the fact that "there is none other name under heaven given among men, whereby we must be saved" (Acts 4:12). Some may see this as applying only to the Christian era, so that before the Christian era God saved men without benefit of Christ. But I prefer to take the verse with complete seriousness. Wherever men have been saved (as was Abraham, for instance), they have been saved by Christ. Since Abraham never heard of Jesus Christ, this may appear absurd. But is it? To be sure, he never heard the name "Jesus Christ." Neither did he ever hear any of the historical data connected with him. But it is not information about Christ that is decisive. It is the person of Christ himself who is the Savior. So we must ask, did Abraham, ignorant of all else, know the *person* whom we call Jesus Christ? I think the answer must be, Yes. For

177

Jesus Christ is the name given to the incarnation of the eternal Son, who was in business long before he took flesh and suffered on the tree. John tells us this in John 1:1. Likewise, Paul tells us this in many places; for instance, in the first chapter of Colossians. There, after giving thanks to God for translating us "into the kingdom of his dear Son" (vs. 13), Paul talks about that "dear Son." In him we have redemption (vs. 14). He is the image of the invisible God (vs. 15). "By him were all things created, that are in heaven, and that are in earth, visible and invisible . . ." (vs. 16). "He is before all things" (vs. 17), and "he is the head of the body, the church" (vs. 18).

What does this mean for Abraham? It would seem to mean that Abraham, in knowing the true God, knew the Son whom we call by his historic name, Jesus Christ. Furthermore, it would seem to suggest that wherever God has operated in self-manifestation, he has done so through the Word, who became flesh in Bethlehem.

If this is true, then I can say—if I understand my terms—that Abraham knew Jesus Christ (to use his historical name) and was saved by him through knowing the triune God—saved by faith, even as we are. Other New Testament passages suggest this truth for other Old Testament saints. Thus we read that Moses esteemed "the reproach of Christ greater riches than the treasures in Egypt" (Heb. 11:26). Finally, Paul insists that the early Israelites "were all baptized unto Moses in the cloud and in the sea; and did all eat the same spiritual meat; and did all drink the same spiritual drink: for they drank of that spiritual Rock that followed them: and that Rock was Christ" (1 Cor. 10:2-4).

There are New Testament passages which actually relate the life of Abraham to the ministry of our Lord. Thus in John 8:56 our Lord says: "Your father Abraham rejoiced to see my day: and he saw it, and was glad." One must not read too much into this passage—as though Abraham was given a vision of a man hanging on a cross for the sins of the world. Paul throws light on just what Abraham "saw" when he writes: "And the scripture, foreseeing that God would justify the heathen through faith, preached before the gospel unto Abraham, saying, In thee shall all nations be blessed" (Gal. 3:8).

I have chosen to use Abraham as an illustration of a man saved by direct confrontation of the one true God and thus by Christ the Son, because his case raises in a special way the problem of heathen who have never heard. Abraham was surrounded by heathen, yet he found the one true God. If it happened once to Abraham, could it happen today to any other man who had never heard the gospel? I think the answer must be, Yes; and again I think we must say that such a man would be saved by Christ—even though in ignorance of the actual name and of the historical information attending the incarnation of the eternal Son. Our conclusion here may be buttressed by recalling that in the biblical history there certainly are glimpses of figures of men outside the bounds of Judaism who knew the true God —Melchizedek, for instance, and Balaam.

But if a man can be saved by direct encounter with the one true God, as Abraham was in his heathen culture, why bother to send missionaries to the heathen? On this question several comments can be made.

For one, we are missionaries for the love of Christ and in obedience to Christ. This in itself would be quite enough to justify the missionary enterprise.

But we can say more. A distinction must be made between one's destiny in the hereafter and salvation in the full New Testament sense. Surely the eternal destiny of Peter, James, and John would have been taken care of had they died through some catastrophe before the death of Christ. But it is quite clear that in spite of this fact, a whole new dimension of God's love and a whole new experience of its power and joy opened to them after Calvary and Pentecost. This made them whole men in a way they had not been before. If it were known that every heathen were to go to heaven at death, it would still be worth his while, during his earthly life, to know Christ in his redemptive fullness.

We can say even more. If a heathen were really in communion with the one true God, as Abraham was, and if he later *did* hear the gospel, or if he *did* read the Bible, he then would acquiesce and immediately respond to it. Missionaries have had this experience. I recall the young Negro boy who ran away from his tribe and who, in the forest, had a real experience of the one true God. A few days later he stumbled into a missionary compound and heard for the first time the story of Jesus and his love. His response was immediate. "I met that God," he cried. "I met him in the forest a few days ago." Missionaries have found men who obviously have been in touch with the Holy Spirit before any missionary ever arrived, men who said on confrontation with the gospel, "I always knew that there was a God like that."

But—and here is the point—such glad response has been a very rare thing in the history of the missionary enterprise. In general, the gospel has been received with scorn or indifference, or more usually with hostility. This shows that these men have been communing, not with the God and Father of our Lord Jesus Christ, but with an idol, an untruth. Those who make such a response are lost. They have not found the true God through direct confrontation, but have suppressed the truth in unbelief. Paul states this in Romans 1:18 and following (where, incidentally, the apostle to the Gentiles makes it clear that God can be known outside the bounds of the historic Christian faith.) Therefore, it is all the more important that the full revelation of God in Christ be proclaimed and that the fullness of God's redemptive love in Christ be offered so that the Holy Spirit may have all the truth to work with in assaulting the hardened hearts of men.

In all this, one thing is quite clear. If a man is saved, as was Abraham, without having ever heard of the historical Christ, it is not *because* of his religion, but *in spite* of it. The theory I am proposing is that a man who has never heard, if he lives up to the light that he does have and thirsts for more, will be led of God step by step out of darkness into the light of his saving presence. This, I take it, is what happened to Abraham.

Reinhold Niebuhr once wrote that we should not be too curious as to the temperature of hell or as to the furniture of heaven. God does not cater to our idle curiosity about many things which are none of our business. We do not know the answer to many questions in which we are interested. But we do know that men are lost, that they need Christ, and that Christ has told us to preach the gospel to every creature. We know yet another thing: That the Judge of all the earth will do what is right. At all costs, we must be sure to present a God who is just, lest we dishonor his Name. This is why Paul is at such pains to insist, in his argument in Romans 1 and 2, that "they are without excuse." The final fault is theirs, and their condemnation cannot be some happenstance which was beyond their control. We must affirm that somehow, somewhere, every man is confronted by the triune God, and that every man has the opportunity to respond.

Perhaps one final comment should be made. I have been suggesting that a man can be saved by the Savior without actually knowing his name or the data connected with his historical mission. Most of us are familiar with at least one group of human beings to which we apply this argument: infants who die before the age of accountability.

Appendix B

THEORIES OF THE ATONEMENT

No theory of the atonement was attempted in Chapter 2 and the matter is touched on only briefly in Chapter 5. The discussion in those chapters, however, should help us to understand something of the history of all such theories.

The three theories of the atonement that have been most famous in the history of the church have arisen from stressing one or another of the three aspects of redemption which have been presented. Thus, one well-known theory, stressing the idea of forgiveness, finds the accused sinner arraigned before the bar of Divine Justice, but pardoned because the penalty was borne by Christ. A second well-known theory is the so-called Dramatic theory. This is sometimes called the Patristic theory. (The word "patristic" here has reference to the period of the early Church Fathers, many of whom were drawn to this theory). It emphasizes the struggle between the forces of God and the forces of evil as being the basic theme of the atonement. A third theory, the Moral Influence theory, stresses the fact that the Cross is the revelation of the love of God, which awakens a corresponding love in us when we comprehend it.

It seems clear that all three of these theories possess merit, though not equal merit; for instance, the Moral Influence theory is notably weak in its view of human sin. Furthermore, these three theories do not exhaust all the ideas that have been proposed in the course of the long history of the church. Yet the varying theories have been but variations on a few general themes.

F. W. Dillistone, in his stimulating book, *The Significance of the Cross,* reduces the themes which have been used to interpret the atonement to four, which are taken
182

from as many different areas of human experience. These four areas of human experience which are used for interpretive purposes are: *a,* that of struggle and conflict—with nature, disease, each other, etc.; *b,* that of the ordering of the life of the community; i.e., the establishment of law, the administration of justice, the maintenance of harmony and peace; *c,* that of the creative experience of men—the construction of useful and beautiful objects, the building up of the institutions of culture, etc.; and *d,* the life of the family. Dillistone insists that within these four areas the whole of human existence is encompassed, and each area, he finds, has been used to interpret the work of Christ. Thus, the Cross has been seen respectively as *a,* redemptive conflict; *b,* righteous judgment; *c;* creative suffering; and *d,* forgiving love. Of these four, *a, b,* and *d,* are illustrated by the three classical theories referred to above. The other, *c,* that of creative suffering, can be brought in line with the exposition in the text as the pattern for our own self-giving service to Christ, in whose sacrificial sufferings we see the creative means by which God is refashioning a universe marred and spoilt by sin.

One interesting aspect of all this is that the early church, with all the councils it called to settle divergent theological issues and with all the resultant creedal statements it was forced to issue to preserve the faith from heresy, never attempted to define an official orthodox theory of the atonement. It was as though human language could only stutter and stammer before the stooping, reconciling grace of a forgiving, redeeming God. Every image we can use, every picture we can draw, but illuminates without explaining the truth that "God was in Christ, reconciling the world unto himself" (2 Cor. 5:19). This truth escapes every verbal net spread out to catch and domesticate it, and goes soaring off into "the wild, blue yonder" of God's eternal mysteries.